Daniel Sörensen

The Automotive Development Process

AF792264

GABLER EDITION WISSENSCHAFT

Daniel Sörensen

The Automotive Development Process

A Real Options Analysis

With a foreword by Prof. Dr. Henry Schäfer

Deutscher Universitäts-Verlag

Bibliografische Information Der Deutschen Nationalbibliothek
Die Deutsche Nationalbibliothek verzeichnet diese Publikation in der Deutschen Nationalbibliografie; detaillierte bibliografische Daten sind im Internet über <http://dnb.d-nb.de> abrufbar.

Dissertation Universität Stuttgart, 2006

D 93

1. Auflage September 2006

Alle Rechte vorbehalten
© Deutscher Universitäts-Verlag | GWV Fachverlage GmbH, Wiesbaden 2006

Lektorat: Brigitte Siegel / Nicole Schweitzer

Der Deutsche Universitäts-Verlag ist ein Unternehmen von Springer Science+Business Media.
www.duv.de

Das Werk einschließlich aller seiner Teile ist urheberrechtlich geschützt. Jede Verwertung außerhalb der engen Grenzen des Urheberrechtsgesetzes ist ohne Zustimmung des Verlags unzulässig und strafbar. Das gilt insbesondere für Vervielfältigungen, Übersetzungen, Mikroverfilmungen und die Einspeicherung und Verarbeitung in elektronischen Systemen.

Die Wiedergabe von Gebrauchsnamen, Handelsnamen, Warenbezeichnungen usw. in diesem Werk berechtigt auch ohne besondere Kennzeichnung nicht zu der Annahme, dass solche Namen im Sinne der Warenzeichen- und Markenschutz-Gesetzgebung als frei zu betrachten wären und daher von jedermann benutzt werden dürften.

Umschlaggestaltung: Regine Zimmer, Dipl.-Designerin, Frankfurt/Main
Druck und Buchbinder: Rosch-Buch, Scheßlitz
Gedruckt auf säurefreiem und chlorfrei gebleichtem Papier
Printed in Germany

ISBN-10 3-8350-0499-9
ISBN-13 978-3-8350-0499-3

Foreword

The global automotive industry is currently undergoing substantial changes in the way firms compete. Driving forces behind these changes are globalized markets, new technologies, and more demanding customers. New structures are evolving within the automotive companies, and there is an increased evidence of the importance of well-functioning networks in order to gain a competitive advantage. The benchmarks for the automotive companies are the demands for higher product quality, more efficiency in bringing products to markets, and a reduction of time to market.

The above changes present the starting point for the research by Daniel Sörensen, which deals with the product development process, in particular within the automobile industry. It is a subject, which up to now hasn't been satisfactorily treated. Daniel Sörensen sets out to explain and value the engineering product development paradigms of point- and set-based concurrent engineering from a holistic viewpoint. First of all, he identifies select capabilities based on empirical studies of best practice in current automotive product development, in particular at Toyota Motor Corporation. This enables a pronounced understanding of why different product engineering systems are able to yield a competitive advantage in the market. Second of all, he applies a real option valuation model to these capabilities within a financial economics framework in order to quantify from the viewpoint of shareholders the value of point- and set-based concurrent engineering processes respectively. In this way, automotive firms are given a powerful tool, which enables them to identify the optimal amount of innovation to build into the product development process. Finally, Daniel Sörensen establishes five clear principles of product development, which give significant direction for automotive executives in designing and controlling the product development process optimally in an uncertain and dynamic environment.

The research by Daniel Sörensen has the potential for a fundamental shift in the way we design and implement product development systems from both the viewpoints of engineering sciences and economics. All in all, based on his superb understanding of the challenge and his ability to combine different viewpoints of the development process, Daniel Sörensen succeeds in developing a pioneering framework for product development, which can aid practitioners as well as academics.

Prof. Dr. Henry Schäfer

Preface

Many thanks to my advisor Prof. Dr. Henry Schäfer for his comments and willingness to take on this work. Special thanks go to Prof. Dr. Hellmuth Milde for his support and helpful insights. I would also like to thank my colleagues Reinhard Ansorge and Gunner Langer for their assistance and plenty of discussions. A deep gratitude goes out to my wonderful wife and best friend Claudia Sörensen. I couldn't have done it without you. I'm also grateful for the process support given by my father-in-law Dr. Hans-Michael Märklin. Thanks in particular to my father Jens Sörensen who convinced me to study finance and provided intellectual stimulation through all the years.

Daniel Jacob Sörensen

Abstract

Executive Summary

The automotive development process ranges from the first idea to the final automotive prototype. Based upon economic theory five principles for value-maximizing the automotive development process are presented. A real options model is developed, which is capable of modeling and valuing in monetary terms the effects of interproject correlation coefficients and volatilities in order to compute the optimal number of designs for elements to develop in parallel.

This thesis presents a novel approach to the automobile development process. It consists of three separate pillars: engineering systems analysis, strategic management analysis, and financial economics. A holistic approach is applied to solving to the problem of how to value, control, and optimize the automobile development process.

Recent research in the worldwide automobile industry as well as research done at Toyota has revealed major differences in the ways automobiles are developed. Two dominant development strategies are identified: point-based and set-based development processes. Point-based development is characterized by a development process where one single design alternative is being developed. Set-based development is characterized by a development process where multiple different design alternatives are being developed concurrently. It is shown that the use of set-based development results in a more extensive process with significant managerial flexibility in an uncertain technical and market environment. The choice between the point- and set-based development strategies is a decision between incurring higher development costs, in order to achieve a higher value of the managerial flexibility to switch between design alternatives dependent on the uncertain environmental outcomes, and the higher incurred investment costs. In other words, set-based development builds-in managerial flexibility to the development process. This flexibility can be extremely valuable for the developing company.

Research within the field of strategic management has shown that the way *how* the developing company chooses to develop its cars significantly influences the competitive advantage of the company and thereby its market value. A framework for identifying and analysing firm-level efficiency advantages in terms of resources, capabilities, and dynamic capabilities is introduced and subsequently applied to the empirical findings from the global automotive industry. Particular emphasis is given to the automotive development process at Toyota. The findings supply evidence for the existence of valuable existing capabilities and dynamic capabilities, which are employed in the development process at Toyota.

It is shown that the financial markets contain much information, which can be utilized in order to value, control, and optimize the automobile development process. A neoclassic approach is utilized in order to specify the valuation models applicable to the automobile development process. In the case of complete markets the utilized valuation model yields a result given by the existence of a unique martingale measure. In the more realistic case of incomplete markets, results can be calculated under the assumption of owners, who are risk-averse to market risks and risk-neutral to private (non-market priced) risks. Given these essential assumptions the automobile development process is shown to correspond to a multivariate contingent claim. The underlyings are the expected present values of the free cash flows resulting from each of the design alternatives being developed concurrently. This novel approach allows for a precise quantitative calculation of the optimal size of the set of design alternatives to be developed concurrently using the set-based development strategy. Subsequently, the value drivers for the contingent claim are identified and analyzed using a sensitivity analysis. Of particular importance for the results are the volatilities of the market and technical uncertainty, the size of the present values of the design alternatives being developed, the correlation structure between the design alternatives, and the size of the investment costs. In practice there is a need for specific capabilities, which allow the management to switch between design alternatives dependent on the technical and market uncertainty. These are shown to be capabilities in platform development, managing sets of design alternatives in parallel, knowing when to narrow the set of alternative design alternatives, and supplier management.

The key result of this thesis is that it is possible to calculate precisely the optimal size of the set of design alternatives to be developed concurrently. Finally, in order to aid the management in the process of valuing, controlling, and optimizing the automotive development process, five principles of automotive development are proposed.

Table of Contents

List of Figures

List of Tables

Glossary of Commonly Used Abbreviations

Abbreviation	*Description*
BEG	Boyle, Evnine, and Gibbs (1989)
BSM	Black, Scholes, and Merton
CAPM	Capital asset pricing model
CCA	Contingent claims analysis
CE	Chief engineer
CEO	Chief executive officer
CSF	Critical success factor
DP	Dynamic programming
E[•]	Expectations operator
ECE	Effective certainty equivalent
ENPV	Extended net present value
FCF	Free cash flow
MAD	Marketed asset disclaimer
NPV	Net present value
PV	Present value
R&D	Research and development
QFD	Quality Function Deployment
RBV	Resource-based view
RBT	Resource-based theory
US	United States

Glossary of Commonly Used Symbols

Symbol	*Description*
A	Automobile design alternative
$\bar{a}_i$	Portfolio weight
B	Automobile design alternative
B_t	Price of bond at time t
C	Automobile design alternative
cov	Covariance
D	Automobile design alternative
DIV	Asset dividend
d	Downward jump size in binomial model
Δ	Delta
$\delta_k(j)$	Boyle, Evnine, and Gibbs (1989) model parameter
$\delta_{km}(j)$	Boyle, Evnine, and Gibbs (1989) model parameter
E	European automobile project
e	Tracking error
$E(\bullet)$	Expectations operator
$E_P(\bullet)$	Expectation under real-world probability measure
$E_Q(\bullet)$	Expectation under martingale probability measure
ε_i	Normally distributed variable with mean 0 and standard deviation 1 in a geometric Brownian motion
F_t	Filtration
f	Price of derivative
h	Length of a time step in a lattice
I_0	Present value of expected investment outlays
$i = 1, 2, \ldots, n$	General index variable

J	Japanese automobile project
K	Number of states of nature ω
λ	Market price of risk
M	Market portfolio
μ_i	Growth rate of asset i in geometric Brownian motion
N	Number of risky assets
n	Sample size in binomial model
$n^*_{\rho_{ij}}$	The optimal number of design alternatives to be developed concurrently given the correlation coefficient ρ_{ij}
Ω	Sample space
$P(\bullet) = p(\bullet)$	Probability
p_P	Probability under real-world measure
p_Q	Probability under martingale measure
Q	Martingale measure
q	Martingale probability
R_F	Risk-free interest rate
r_t	Discount rate at time t
R_i	Return on asset i
R_M	Return on market portfolio
ρ_{ij}	Correlation coefficient between i and j
$\sigma = \sigma_i$	Standard deviation of variable i (in the case of a normal distribution); the second moment of the probability distribution of i (in the general case)
$S_i(t, \omega) = S_i$	Price of risky asset i in state of nature ω
$t_i = t$	Time
T	$T \in t$, End point in time
$\binom{t}{n}$	Binomial coefficient

U	U.S. automobile project
u	Upward jump size in binomial model
V_t	Value of trading strategy at time t
ω_i	State of nature
$\Psi(\omega)$	State price
W; W_N	Financial claim; Duplicating portfolio
X	Automotive development strategy
$X(\omega)$	Pure-state claim; Arrow-Debreu security
Y	Automotive development strategy
Z_t	Martingale variable

Chapter 1: Introduction

The global automotive industry is currently undergoing significant changes, which in turn is creating new opportunities as well as new threats for the involved companies. At the same time the importance of the automotive industry as seen in its link to employment numbers and the amounts invested in research and development continues to dominate the national economies (Wolfe 2005, p. 3). Traditional automotive industry giants such as General Motors, Ford Motor Company, Volkswagen, and DaimlerChrysler are currently fighting furiously to even maintain their market share and profitability. At the same time Asian automotive companies, predominantly Toyota Motor Corporation, are gaining market share and profitability at high rates (KPMG 2006). All this begs for a renewed answer to the age-old question:

How can automotive companies continue to win the hearts and minds of their future customers?

The answer to the above question was, is, and will be: innovation. The core notion underlying this answer is the liberalistic principle of free markets. Adam Smith's "invisible hand" (Smith 1976) and Joseph Schumpter's "creative destruction" (Schumpeter 1950) are simultaneously the driving forces for change and also point towards the solution: Management at the automotive companies must be able (and willing) to put the customer first, in every aspect of its objectives, strategies, and business processes.

In recent years the rate of globalization has increased rapidly. Some of the vehicles of change have been the increased importance of international trade, financial markets, and the establishment of supranational political organs to further the progress. From an economics perspective the structural changes have tended to increase volatility and result in a difficulty of prognosing future developments. This is particularly felt by the decision-makers in the automobile industry according to a recent study (KPMG 2006).

This leads to a pronounced need for newer and improved business models. The majority of respondents in the KPMG study list the following initiatives as being the currently most significant: adaptive and lean manufacturing systems, new product materials, outsourcing, etc. (KPMG 2006). These all represent interesting and sometimes valuable suggestions. Still, the importance of the product development process is seen in the way it is constitutive of innovation. It embodies the core ideas of the organization and its long term *raison d'être*. In MacDuffie and Benko (2006, p. 2) the current state of the global automotive industry is summed up in the words: "Given the competitive intensity of this industry, if your products aren't innovative, you won't attract customers." Unfortunately, the process of innovation is difficult to analyze and predict. If it were possible to present a model by which innovation is guaranteed then all companies could duplicate it and any resulting competitive advantage is erased. The result would be perfect competition and would imply a rather mechanistic approach to business management. If managed properly, few would disagree; the development process would lead to a competitive advantage in the market.

This thesis is concerned with the automotive development process and is particularly directed at automobile managers and academics, who are looking for a holistic approach, involving the areas of systems engineering, strategic management, and financial economics, to optimizing the automobile development process. Based on empirical research concerning the automobile development process in a wide variety of companies, two basic models for the development process (point-based and set-based concurrent engineering) are identified and compared. The models are then analyzed from the viewpoint of strategic management in order to identify efficiency advantages stemming from different approaches to managing key business processes. These business processes are then valued utilizing valuation models from financial economics. The purpose is to be able to prescribe an optimal approach to managing the automobile development process.

This thesis has the following main research characteristics:

1) It employs a holistic approach to making recommendations. The presented models within the fields of engineering systems analysis, strategic management analysis, and financial economics are seen as complementary to solving the challenge of optimizing the automobile development process.

2) The challenge to optimizing the automobile development process is essentially reduced to the question of how much managerial flexibility to build into the automobile development process. Modelling managerial flexibility explicitly, it is shown that the volatilities and the correlations between the design alternatives can be taken advantage of within the development process. This leads to the conclusion of a "portfolio effect" in the automobile development process. This is a major contribution of this work and provides the basis for future research.

3) The resulting optimal resource allocation has a major relevance for the relationship management between the automotive developing companies and their suppliers. It can be shown quantitatively that there is a high value-added in being able to incorporate the skills of competent suppliers in the automobile development process.

4) The concept of modularity is viewed in a new framework. Modularity namely provides the technical foundation for working in sets of design alternatives in parallel. Very successful companies such as Toyota are utilizing this approach, and the economic rationale and assumptions underlying this approach are discussed within the before mentioned valuation model.

The next page presents the problem statement for the thesis and an elaboration thereof. Subsequently, the thesis is delimited. Finally, the methodology for the thesis is introduced and argued for.

1.1 Problem Statement

The objective of this research will be to solve the following primary problem:

How is it possible to value, control, and optimize the automotive product development process?

In order to answer this question the following subproblems[i] will be sought answered:

1. What are the key characteristics of the automotive development process and what models of design are available for the development process?
2. What role does the automotive development process play in helping the developing company attain a sustainable competitive advantage in the marketplace?
3. What are the relevant real options available to management in the development process, and how are these valued from the perspective of the developing company?
4. How can management structure the development process in order to maximize its value?

[i] See Leedy (1980, p. 57) for a discussion of the use of subproblems in solving a main problem piecemeal.

Elaboration on Problem Statement

The above problems will now be elaborated on:

AD. "Primary problem":
The research object of the thesis is the automotive development process. The aspects of "valuation" and "control" are perfectly correlated, in that any action with an effect on cash flows will automatically affect the value of the development process. Therefore, control and valuation must be solved simultaneously. The final aspect of "optimization" involves maximizing the value of the development process by identifying an optimal development process setup.

AD. "Subproblem 1":
First of all, the purpose of this subproblem is to present and analyze the automotive development process as the primary unit of analysis for the following research. The automotive development process is depicted as an interrelated system of development decisions. Special attention is, therefore, given to the decisions and events, which significantly affect the system-wide development effort. Second of all, various models for automotive development are presented, and their key assumptions and performance are compared.

AD. "Subproblem 2":
This subproblem seeks to relate the automotive development process to the corporate goal of creating and sustaining a competitive advantage in the marketplace. First of all, the two primary views of strategic management analysis, strategic fit and strategic stretch, are presented and compared as to their fundamental assumptions and characteristics. Second of all, the automotive development process is analyzed as to how management can use it to attain a strategic fit and strategic stretch. Particular emphasis is given to empirical analyses of how individual automotive companies derive a competitive advantage from their automotive development process.

AD. "Subproblem 3":

The purpose of this subproblem is to identify and compare the various forms of managerial flexibility in the automotive development process using a real option valuation model. First of all, the role of financial markets and the assumptions for modelling real options are discussed in terms of general valuation principles. Second of all, a specific real option model capable of valuing the automotive development process is developed and discussed.

AD. "Subproblem 4":

The purpose of this subproblem is to analyze the automobile development process taken as a whole, in order to maximize its value for the developing company. The primary tool for answering this problem will be the valuation model of the automobile development process developed with regard to subproblem 3. In order to find an optimal development process, the model is utilized to analyze and compare the value of various development process compositions.

1.2 Delimitation

In answering the problem statement, the thesis will be delimited by the following points:

- The object of analysis is the automobile development process. The preceding research process and the following production process are not examined explicitly. On the input side of the automotive development process a given technology freezer is assumed given. The management challenge considered in the current work is related to optimize the use of these technologies within the scope of the development process. Likewise the output side of the development process is assumed to be consistent with the outcome of the automotive development process.
- Organizational theory regarding organizational structure and individual behaviour plays a potentially important role in shedding light on the development process. The influence on the development process will be mentioned and briefly discussed when appropriate. Elsewhere the assumption is made that the individuals participating in the development process are working in the best interests of the owners of the developing company. This assumption allows the emphasis to be on the information processing taking place during the automobile development process.[2]
- Technical complexities play an equally important role in the development process. From an engineering perspective, various technical details regarding the automotive product to be developed may be in the foreground. In this thesis, technical details and specifications will be mentioned and discussed when appropriate. Elsewhere the emphasis will be placed on the main characteristics of the automotive product and technically detailed product and process aspects will be refrained from.

---

[2] Clark and Fujimoto (1991, pp. 18-22) make a similar assumption in their empirical research of the world auto industry.

1.3 Methodology

This section deals with the methodology (see, e.g., Brodbeck 1968, Morison 1993, and Davis and Parker 1997) for the thesis. The purpose is to provide a basic reasoning for the applied approach to solving the main problem of the thesis. In general, the discipline of business administration will provide a setting for solving the main problem. As such, the focus is on maximizing the market value of the company. This is a natural application of the liberalistic economic principles, which let free market forces influence the resource allocation in the economy as a whole, as well as at the level of the individual company.

1.3.1 Theoretical Basis

The main problem of the thesis deals with the automotive development process. Because the development process touches on much of what a company does, it is only natural to start with a broader theoretical view. This is accomplished by viewing the automotive development process from both the viewpoint of the engineering sciences[3] as well as from the business administration viewpoint[4]. In other words, the theoretical basis for the thesis is purposefully chosen to be broad. The theories originate mainly in the subjects of engineering, strategic management, and financial economics. In solving the main problem, the emphasis is placed on the theories of finance. Particular importance is given to the theory of real options, as this theory has the potential to develop new insights into the management of the automotive development process. The theory of real options will form the main theoretical backbone of the arguments later in the thesis.

1.3.2 Data Basis

The data basis of the thesis consists of both quantitative as well as qualitative data. From the above-mentioned theories, the theories and models from strategic

---

[3] This is primarily done in answering subproblem 1 of the problem statement.

[4] This is primarily done in answering subproblems 2 to 4 of the problem statement.

management are based primarily on qualitative data. The theories and models from engineering and business administration are based primarily on quantitative data. As particular emphasis is placed on the theory of real options, and the main problem of the thesis deals among other things with the important aspect of valuation, the major source of data will be quantitative data.

The thesis is mainly based on secondary data (quantitative and qualitative). These are drawn from the literature, which deals with the automotive development process and strategic management in general. Apart from specific primary data, which is indeed of high relevance for developing recommendations in practice, the emphasis in this thesis is on employing a deductive approach based on hypothetical data. To start with various assumptions and models are described and presented. Applying deductive arguments augmented with hypothetical data for illustrative purposes, conclusions are then drawn. I.e., the contribution of this thesis is in developing the models, which could later applied in practice. This has an important consequence for the analysis in the thesis. Calculations in the analysis are based almost exclusively on hypothetical data. The importance of the specific (more or less realistic) numbers is secondary to the overarching aim of generating the framework to be used in solving the main problem. Placed on a timeline, the work in this thesis is prior to possible positivistic empirical research, which could be carried out in order to validate the models presented on the following pages.

1.3.3 Reliability and Validity

Having discussed and delimitated the theoretical and data basis of the thesis it is now fitting to discuss the crucial aspects of reliability and validity in relation to the applied methodology. The terms are illustrated in Figure 1.

Figure 1: Reliability and Validity

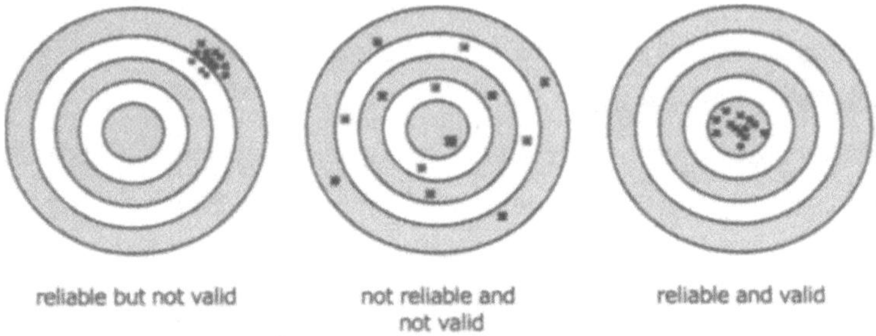

Source: Linn and Gronlund (2000, p. 75)

The reliability of the thesis depends on its ability to "produce the same answer in the same circumstances, time after time" (Johnson and Harris 2002, pp. 102-103). This corresponds to the left bullseye in Figure 1. The above stated use of theoretical (quantitative) models primarily from the subject of financial economics and the use of quantitative data both ensure a high degree of reliability for the thesis. E.g., option pricing models always yield the same results given a fixed set of inputs. The use of models from strategic management has a somewhat lower reliability due to the qualitatively based line of argumentation. This is a consequence of the nature of the subject strategic management. E.g., it is difficult to mathematically prove the strategic importance of a specific business process given a fixed set of inputs to the model. In general the strategic management literature employs a wide variety of terms and definitions for some objects, which are closely related. In order to avaoid confusion and thereby enhance the reliability of the thesis, the models from strategic management are enhanced by the use of stringent definitions of terms and definitions in order to present univocal arguments.

The discussion about reliability is a part of the discussion regarding the validity of the thesis. Validity[5] deals with whether the thesis "actually measures what it is purported to measure" (Johnson and Harris 2002, p. 103). As such, it is not possible to have high validity without at the same time having high reliability. E.g., if there is no reliability and no validity in the thesis, this corresponds to the centre bullseye in Figure 1. In other words, validity is the ultimate "benchmark" for the quality of the presented research.

In order to make this thesis correspond as much as possible to the right bullseye in Figure 1, much deliberation has been made in order to ensure a high degree of validity. First, as mentioned above, the theoretical basis of thesis is purposefully broad to start with. This is to ensure that the analysis of the thesis is framed in terms of both qualitative and quantitative models and ultimately qualitative and quantitative performance drivers. The automotive development process is both in theory and in practice much too complex to be analyzed overall with a quantitative model alone. Therefore, a theoretically as well as empirically valid analysis of the automotive development process in principle incorporates both qualitative and quantitative variables. In this thesis, the qualitative models from strategic management and engineering serve as a check to the validity of the quantitative model setup from financial economics, which is used as a primary instrument in the analysis.

Second, the validity of the thesis is enhanced by a mixture of deductive and inductive line of argumentation. Deductive arguments are mainly applied when constructing arguments in the analysis based on assumptions, on previous results, or on established models from theory. This is to ensure a sound theoretical basis for the thesis.[6] In this way, the thesis builds upon and adds to existing theory by arguing for new and important causalities. Inductive arguments are mainly applied when given aspects are generalized to be relevant for the analysis. This is primarily so when various case studies and research from the automotive industry are presented. In this regard the

[5] Strictly speaking, validity in this context is equivalent to so-called „external validity". Refer to Leedy (1990, p. 37) for a discussion of external validity.

[6] The theoretical basis of thesis is discussed above.

validity of the thesis depends on two factors. The first factor, which influences the validity of the thesis, is the reliability and validity of the individual works. The second factor is the degree to which the objects of analysis in the respective works can be transferred to the current problem at hand. In other words, this implies a discussion about the validity of the secondary data for the thesis. In addition, the choice of mainly quantitative modelling applied to the automotive development process is vulnerable to both the assumptions regarding the causalities implied in the models as well as the lack of quantitative and financial market data, which would be applicable to the valuation of the automotive development process.

Chapter 2: The Automotive Development Process

The purpose of this chapter is to deal mainly with answering subproblem 1 of the problem statement:
What are the key characteristics of the automotive development process and what models of design are available for the development process?

The overall purpose of this chapter is to set the frame for the subsequent analysis of the automobile development process. First of all, because the automobile is the central product of the development process, it is introduced and some basic characteristics and objectives of the automobile and the development process are outlined. Second of all, this chapter deals specifically with the automotive development process and characterizes it as a system of interrelated decisions and events. The purpose is to outline how the development process can be characterized as a complex decision-making process under uncertainty. Finally, three current automotive development models are introduced and subsequently compared in terms of their structure, impact on decision-making, and performance characteristics. The purpose is to identify and perform a preliminary analysis of the value drivers in the automotive development process. The three models will in subsequent chapters serve as the main paradigms of automobile development, which management must choose between.

2.1 The Setting of the Automobile Development Process

The present-day automobile consists of up to 20,000 separate components (Liker et al. 1996, p. 168). There are therefore roughly 400 million possible interactions between the components.[7] This product complexity is compounded by a multitude of factors within

[7] 20,000 x (20,000 – 1) = 399,980,000

and outside the developing organization. The process of developing an automobile could, therefore, be a voluminous task.

In their work dealing with product development Clark and Fujimoto (1991) rank a product in general along two dimensions: internal and external complexity (see Figure 2). Internal complexity is determined by e.g., the number of unique components, production process, internal product interfaces, and nature of technological trade-offs between the components. External complexity is determined by e.g., the quantity and types of performance criteria, and extent to which the customer emphasizes measurable and/or subtle dimensions of the product.

Figure 2: Internal and External Product Complexity

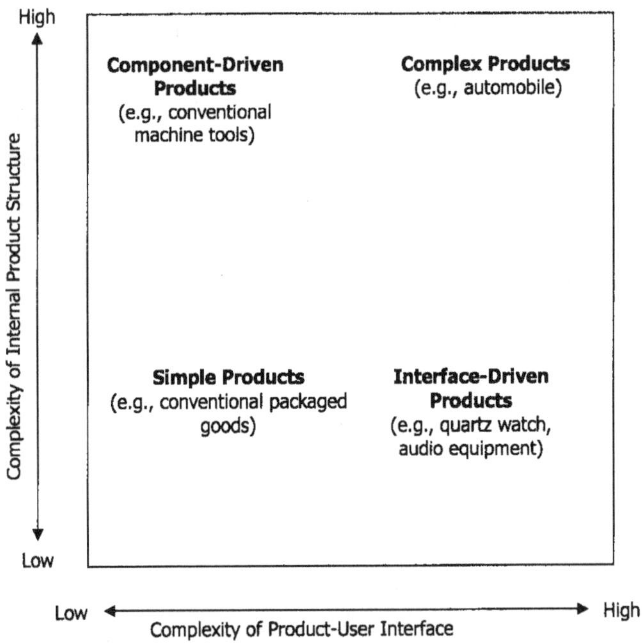

Source: Clark and Fujimoto (1991, p. 11)

The product (the automobile) in focus of this thesis is located in the upper right quadrant of the product complexity grid and thereby belongs to the group of the most complex products. As such, the automobile can be characterized by both a high degree of external as well as internal complexity. E.g., the many different and sometimes technologically advanced components (such as electronic systems) require careful attention from management because they have the potential to greatly influence the characteristics of the final automobile. Likewise the customer interacts with the automobile along many different dimensions, which must all be considered by management. In practice the product complexity (internal and external) of the automobile makes "coordination of the total vehicle extremely challenging" (Clark and Fujimoto 1991, p. 10). The complexity of the final automobile accordingly also influences the development thereof. Clark and Fujimoto (1991, p. 112) liken the development of a car to solving a huge simultaneous equation system. This characteristic has significant implications for the thesis as the description and subsequent analysis of the automotive development process is exposed to the underlying complexity of the automobile. The challenge lies in identifying and subsequently analyzing the key performance drivers of the automotive development process. Indeed, Schwartz (2002, p. 4) states: "The analysis of R&D projects is one of the most difficult investment problems," and the decisions made during the product development process have a significant impact on the total costs involved in bringing a car to the market. An often cited statistic is that as much as 80% of the total automotive product costs are determined by the decisions made during the development process (see Jaikumar 1986 and Soderberg 1989). Managing the automotive development process efficiently is therefore an important corporate performance driver.

As stated in the main problem of the problem statement the focus of the thesis is on the important aspect of valuation. In order to value a given setup of the automotive development process it is necessary to analyze the automotive decision-making process in terms of its impacts on the cash flows and risk structures in the development process. The following outline of the automotive development process serves as a basis among other things for the subsequent valuation model of the development process. Hence, the complexity of the automobile and its development has a decisive impact. Any valid valuation model of the automotive development process must represent and describe the essential resulting cash flows and risk structures of the development process. The identification of the before-mentioned key performance drivers are here of utmost relevance for valuation purposes. This is no simple task.[8] Due to the complexity of the product and the resulting challenges in the development phase there is therefore a need for a framework in this chapter, which would be able to capture the main effects on cash flows and risk. This aspect shall serve as an underlying motive for the rest of the chapter.

2.2 The Automotive Development Process

To start with, the overall aims of the automobile development process are pointed out and discussed. Wheelwright and Clark (1992) mention three imperatives (see Figure 3) for the automobile development process.[9]

Figure 3: Three Imperatives of the Automobile Development

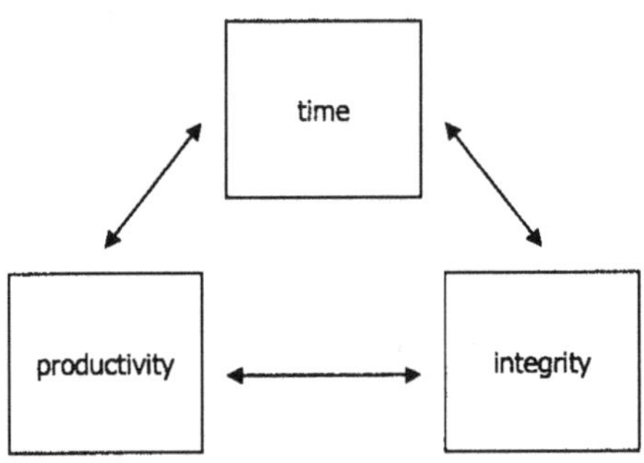

Source: adapted from Wheelwright and Clark (1992)

[8] The actual valuation model is developed and presented in chapter 4.

[9] Similarly, Clark and Fujimoto (1991) list three objectives: Total product quality, lead time, and productivity.

In other words, any automotive development process should have as objectives to develop the car as quickly as possible (i.e., the variable "time"), utilize the invested resources as efficiently as possible (i.e., the variable "productivity"), and finally to develop the car to match or exceed the customers' requirements (i.e., the variable "integrity").[10] These objectives are related to value of the automotive development process as they are linked to the timing and size of the resulting cash flows. The objectives are neither independent nor necessarily fixed. Rather, they are influenced by the employed development process. It is this process, which shall now be dealt with more extensively.

In the literature, the automotive development process is mostly depicted as linear due to the sequential structure of decision-making. I.e., the decision(s) taken at time t influence the set of decisions available at time $t+1$.[11] Regarding the specific course of actions contained in the development process, various authors list somewhat different generic product development processes, but they all share the same basic structure. Differences are given by the level of detail covered. One such generic development process is presented in Ulrich and Eppinger (2000) who list five major phases (see Figure 4).

[10] Chapter 3 deals more extensively with these objectives and their implications from the viewpoint of strategic management.

[11] Note that taking no decision at time t is also a decision (a potentially very valuable decision as will be discussed in chapter 4 and chapter 5).

Figure 4: The Five Phases of Product Development

1. Concept development
   ⇩
2. System-level design
   ⇩
3. Detail design
   ⇩
4. Testing and refinement
   ⇩
5. Production ramp-up

Source: adapted from Ulrich and Eppinger (2000)

The above phases will now be briefly elaborated on. The first phase (concept development) has the needs of the target market (i.e., the customer(s)) as a starting point. Hereupon one or more concepts are developed and tested. Ulrich and Eppinger (2000, p. 17) define the concept as "a description of the form, function, and features of a product". The second phase (system-level design) is the first of two product design phases. It deals with the overall automobile product architecture and as such engages in the definition of subsystems, their specifications, and the interfaces between them. The output of the second phase is a geometric layout of the automobile. The third phase (detail design) complements the previous phase in respect to the completeness of the overall design specifications. In this second product design phase the specifications of the car are developed to such a degree that production of all the unique parts in the automobile can take place. The fourth phase (testing and refinement) is involved with constructing prototypes in order to test the developed automobile according to customer requirements. The fifth and final phase (production ramp-up) precedes the official product launch (and mass production). This final phase marks simultaneously a major commitment by the production function and the official end of the development process. Figure 4 shows a development process following a sequential setup with phase *i* starting upon completion of phase *i*-1. This depiction has been chosen mainly for illustrative purposes. In practice, there are three aspects of this illustration, which need to be mentioned. First, one or more of the phases could be taking place simultaneously. Second, the phases are most likely to be interdependent. I.e., not only is there a vertical arrow in a downward direction, but there is also one or more in an upward direction. The net result is a development process characterized by one or more loops. There are in principle an unlimited number of possible loops as well as number of times that each loop can be entered into.[12] Third, the role of information is just as important as the development of the actual (physical) automobile. One might imagine a parallel vertical process in Figure 4, which is linked to the development of the automobile, and involves the creation and management of information.

In their extensive research on the world automobile industry Clark and Fujimoto (1991) present a model (see Figure 5) for the automotive product development process, which incorporates the aspect of information into the development process. Figure 5 consists of three interlinked processes: the product development process, the production process, and the consumption process.[13] The product development process is very similar in its setup to the generic development process presented in Figure 4. "System-level design" and "Detail design" in Figure 4 are comparable to "Product plan" and "Product design" respectively in Figure 5. The "Testing and refinement" phase in Figure 4 has been relegated to the respective testing activities, which take place during the course of each stage in Figure 5. The "Production process" in Figure 5 is a continuation of the "Production ramp-up" phase in Figure 4. The consumption process represents the customer's experience with the automobile once it has been produced. During this phase, a distinction is made between "existing" and "potential" customers, as both groups need to be taken into consideration.

---

[12] The term "loop" is later in this chapter understood as one or more "design-build-test" cycles.

[13] Of the three mentioned processes, the product development process is the primary focus of this thesis.

Figure 5: The Development Process as an Information System

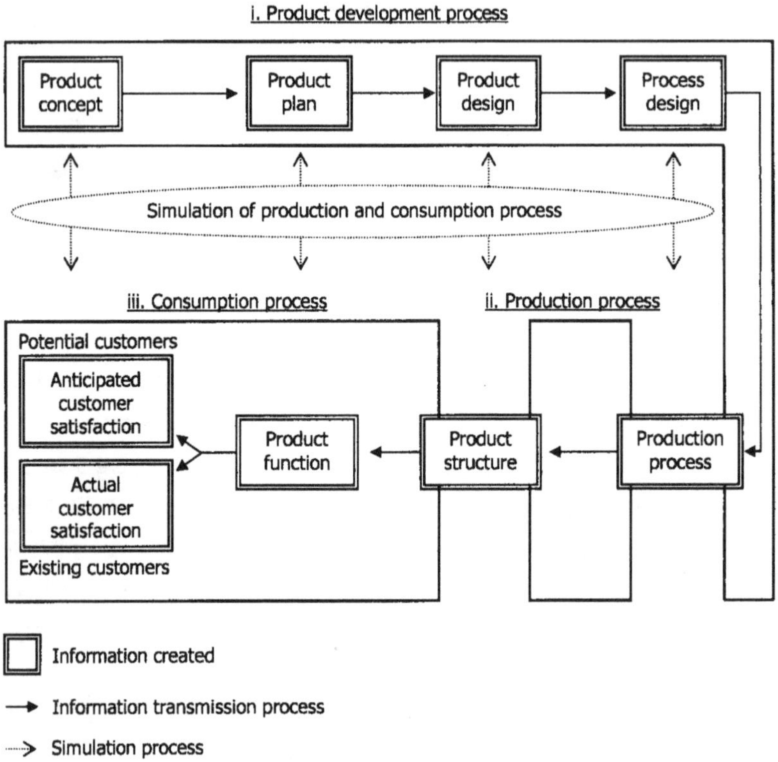

Source: adapted from Clark and Fujimoto (1991, p. 23)

The focus of Figure 5 is on the information generation and subsequent transmission occurring in and between the stages. Information is created and communicated as the automotive design progresses during the development process. Information is also needed to produce the car in the production process. During the consumption process, the customers receive information about the product from interaction with the product. From stage to stage, the set of information therefore is enlarged.

The key to understanding the progression of the automotive design lies in the centre of Figure 5. Here the automotive development process is understood as a simulation of the future production and consumption process. In other words, the individual steps in the upper part of Figure 5 (i.e., the development process) basically parallel (shown by the vertical punctuated arrows) the corresponding steps in the lower part of the figure (i.e., the production and consumption processes). Due to the simulation process management can compare the current state of the automotive design to various simulated and potential outcomes. The information generated by the simulation process at the various points in time is, therefore, central to optimizing the development process. During the "Product concept" phase engineers are basically concerned with anticipating and incorporating the customers' (existing and potential) future product satisfaction into the product. The phase "Product plan" envisions the styling, layout, and major platform related characteristics of the future automobile in order to achieve the desired product functions. Likewise, the phase "Product design" deals with the development all of the technical details of the future automobile. Finally, the phase "Process design" parallels the actual shop-floor production by developing factory designs, production equipment design, and standard operating procedures. As such, the product development effort both starts and ends with the customer. In other words, the market (the customer) is the ultimate appraiser of the company's development effort.

The information perspective shifts the emphasis from the actual physical product (the automobile) to the information needed to develop it. It is the information about events and technical developments throughout the developing organization, which management can utilize in order to manage the multitude of interdependencies during the development process. The information perspective is therefore focused on managing the linkages in the development process. One of the objectives by managing these linkages is to be able to develop an automobile with a high degree of integrity (see Figure 3). There are two value drivers, which both deal with managing linkages and determine the integrity of the developed automobile. These are external and internal integrity. External integration deals with how well the developed automobile fits the customer's requirements, e.g., how well the car's style and interior layout satisfies the customer. Internal integrity deals with how well the functions of the product are matched by its structure, e.g., how well the parts fit and work together in order to achieve a certain degree of safety in crash tests. In summary, Figure 3 shows that the challenge in the automotive development process is for management to design and manage a development process, which produces a car of high internal and external integrity and at the same time does this quickly and efficiently. This is one of the central themes in a large number of scientific articles focused on automobile product development performance.

In order to understand the automobile development process altogether it is useful to view the development process as taking place in a "design space". Coyne et al. (1990) employ this concept with the purpose of creating a theoretical framework to discuss the process of improving the automobile design. Ward et al. (1995, p. 52) state: "for any given design problem, there is a true, yet unknown, 'design space' that includes all possible values for all the parameters." An example of the design space is illustrated in Figure 6.

Figure 6: The Design Space

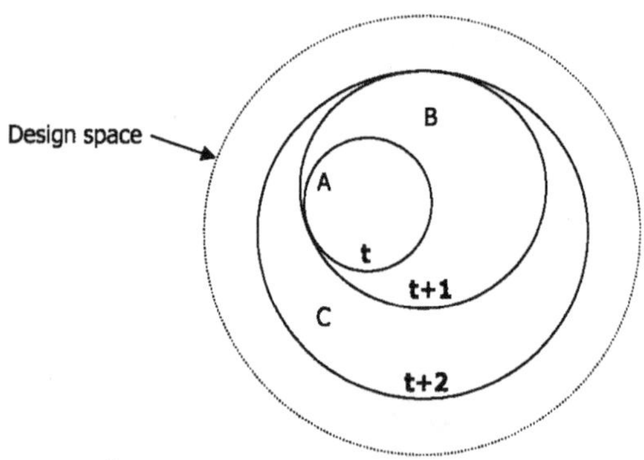

Source: own creation

In Figure 6 are illustrated three sets of designs *t*, *t*+1, and *t*+2 (all inside the true, yet unknown, design space). Each set represents the feasible designs, which the developing company is considering, at three successive points in time. At time *t* the company is

contemplating the design *A*. The design characterizes a unique combination of design parameters, which is different in at least one parameter from other feasible designs. At time *t*+1 the developing company has extended its search for an optimal design to include the design *B*. At the next point in time (*t*+2) the design *C* is examined. The goal for the developing company is to map out the various feasible designs in order to compare these to each other as there exist combinations of design parameters, which are more optimal than others are. Within the concept of the design space the automobile development process becomes a problem-solving process of searching through a state space. "Problem" in this context is understood as a difference between the current state of the automotive design and a more optimal design. A very important characteristic of this search process is the existence of uncertainty. I.e., it is not known with certainty (100%) what will be the outcome of the search process.
At the core of the problem-solving process is the design-build-test cycle (refer in general to Coyne et al. 1990) illustrated in Figure 7.

Figure 7: The Design-Build-Test Cycle

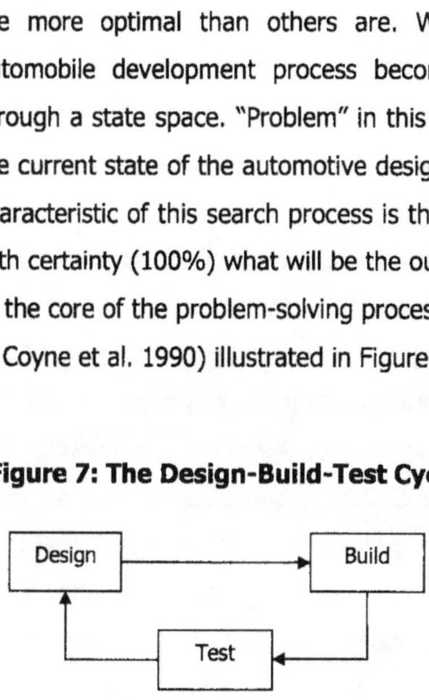

Source: Own creation

The design-build-test cycle is based on an iterative view of design. It starts with a given combination of design parameters. Then a prototype of the design is constructed, and finally the prototype is tested. The outcome of the test is then compared to the objectives for the design. As previously mentioned these are to achieve internal and external integrity. Specifically the design is evaluated according to how well it simulates the production and consumption processes (see Figure 5). If there is a discrepancy between the current design and the objectives, management can opt to modify the design and start the cycle again (this time with the modified design). The result of this reiteration is that the design increases in detail after each cycle. This corresponds to various designs being evaluated at successive points in time (see Figure 6). In the same way, the design-build-test cycle is the main contributor to the generation of information from stage to stage in Figure 5. Portrayed in this manner the design-build-test cycle can be viewed as the most elemental building block of the automotive development process. Like the automotive development process, the design-build-test cycle can be benchmarked according to the three criteria listed in Figure 3. Therefore, if one wishes to optimize the automotive development process, a cardinal objective is to master the design-build-test cycle.

As mentioned above, a key activity in the design-build-test cycle (and therefore also in the automotive development process) is the construction of prototypes. The prototype embodies the current state of the automotive design and can be depicted as one of the design alternatives in the design space (see Figure 6). By itself, it is a stand-in for the car (or a part of it) to be mass-produced. It represents the information available to management about the automotive design and is an information-generating asset as the current state of information can be updated after each design-build-test cycle. That is to say, the design-build-test cycle is concerned with one prototype (one alternative in the design space) at time t, and the subsequent updating by the management of the information set (the design specification) represents the next alternative (prototype) in the design space at time $t+1$. The prototype is therefore both a technical tool as well as a key management tool for managing information about the development effort. Wheelwright and Clark (1992, pp. 255-256) testify to the importance of prototyping: "Senior managers, functional heads, project leaders who do not understand and fully utilize the power of prototyping unintentionally handicap their efforts to achieve rapid, effective, and productive development results."

Due to the importance of managing prototypes a brief overview of various prototype forms is given. Wheelwright and Clark (1992) catalog four main forms of prototypes: simulation, mockups, functional products, and pilot production (see Table 1).

Table 1: Forms of Prototypes

Prototype form	*Examples*	*Time*	*Cost*	*Final Product Resemblance*
1. Simulation	• Computer Aided Design modeling • Finite element analysis • Heat transfer approximations	low	low	low
2. Mockups	• Styrofoam block models • Parts made through stereolitography	low	low	low
3. Functional products	• First-unit circuit board • Engineering-built engines • Pre-production products	medium	medium	medium
4. Pilot production	• Prototype with very high resemblance to the product for mass production	high	high	high

Source: Own creation, adapted from Wheelwright and Clark (1992)

Simulation mostly takes place using a computer program, which can help the engineer explore the design as a virtual object relatively quickly. Mockups represent the next level of prototypes. They are physical prototypes, which look like the product. Functional prototypes not only look like the product (or part of it) but are also meant to work like it. These prototypes are more extensive, normally cost more, and take longer to build. Pilot production prototypes bear a very high resemblance to the actual product for mass production, i.e., the final automotive design. During the development of a car, the standard progression is to start with simulations and mockups and only later in development use the functional prototypes when the design has become more mature. Pilot production prototypes are normally preceded by one or more of the other prototype forms. At large one could say that the costs of prototyping and the development phase (time) are inversely related (see Figure 8).

Figure 8: The Costs of Prototyping

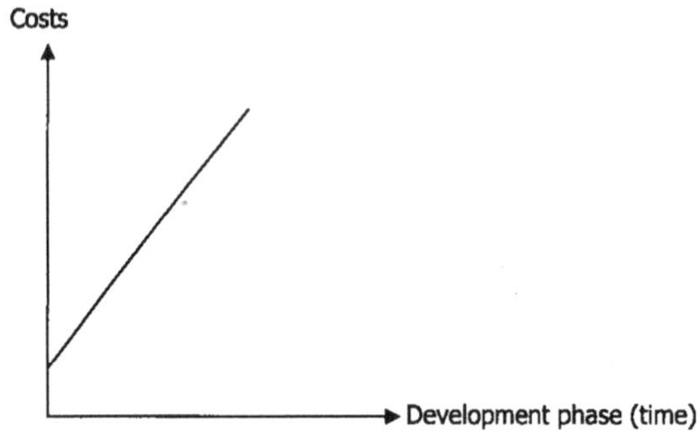

Source: Own creation

For reasons of simplicity, the relationship in Figure 8 is shown to be linear. The actual relationship would have to be examined empirically. For the purpose of this thesis, a theoretical positive correlation between time and costs (see Table 1) shall be presumed because the development costs rise as a consequence of primarily the investments in the increasingly realistic prototypes and the assets needed to produce them. Therefore, the prototyping costs are most likely variable in nature and are greater when more prototypes are built.

As pointed out earlier the purpose of the development process is to create an automobile with a high degree of integrity (external and internal). Prototyping (the design-build-test cycle) plays a dominant role in this respect and also has high internal and external integrity as the objective. The prototype serves a dual purpose and should ideally both incorporate the customer's requirements and at the same time perform well from a technical point of view. Due to the complexity of the automobile (see Figure 2), the dynamics of the marketplace, and the technical developments, external and internal requirements are not only difficult to capture using the prototype, but they also change constantly. The search through design space (see Figure 6) can be forced by unforeseen developments either internally or externally. Management must therefore use the prototype to react and accommodate to these uncertainties. Presuming managerial flexibility to react, uncertainty does not only have a negative impact on the value of the development process, because management has the possibility of actively shaping the development process. Throughout the automobile development process, information is generated and the automotive design is optimized. As a consequence the degree of technical uncertainty is decreasing with time. The automotive design matures due to the increasing number of design-build-test cycles, and there are accordingly less unsolved technical issues compared to the beginning of the development process. Figure 9 depicts this relationship.

Figure 9: Technical Uncertainty and Prototyping

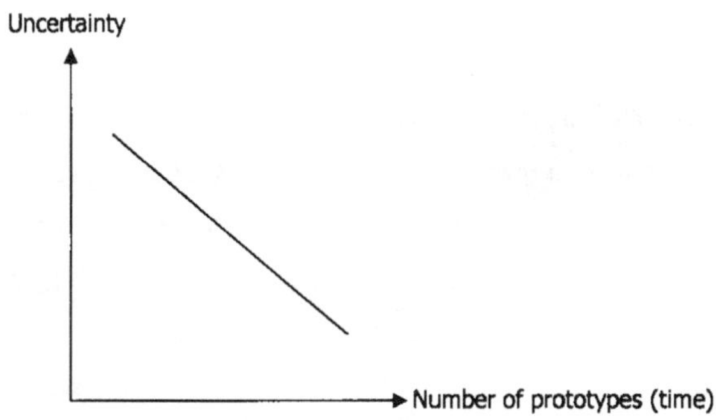

Source: Own creation

For reasons of simplicity, the graph above is assumed linear, and a negative correlation between time and technical uncertainty shall be presumed.

2.3 Present Value Method for the Automotive Development Process

At this point it is purposeful to briefly explain the concept of valuation in the context of the automobile development process. The subject of valuation is central to this work, as stated in the problem statement, and is a topic, which shall be explored more in depth in chapters 4 and 5. The are several investment valuation methods, but the most commonly accepted model of valuation is the present value method stated in equation (2.1) (see, e.g., Brealey, Myers, and Allen 2005).

(2.1) $$\text{NPV}=-I_0+\text{PV}(\text{FCF})=-I_0+\sum_{t=1}^{n}\frac{\text{E}(\text{FCF}_t)}{(1+r_t)^t}$$

where

NPV = Net Present Value

I_0 = Investment Costs at time 0

PV = Present Value

FCF_t = The Expected Free Cash Flow at time t

r_t = Discount rate at time t

The present value method basically consists of three components. The first is the FCF, which is the cash return resulting from a given object, e.g., an automotive development process, at time t. The second is r_t, which is the discount rate to be applied to the FCF at time t. It represents the opportunity costs of the invested capital I_0, which is the third component of the present value method. The PV represents the value, which an investor would assign to the object and therefore the price, which the investor would maximally be willing to currently pay for the object. Therefore, if the present value of the expected cash flows exceeds the size of the investment outlay, the present value method prescribes that the investor should invest in the object, and it has a positive NPV. If the present value of the expected cash flows equals the size of the investment outlay, the present value method prescribes that the investor is indifferent towards the object, and it has 0 NPV. If the present value of the expected cash flows doesn't exceed the size of the investment outlay, the present value method prescribes that the investor should refrain from investing in the object, and it has negative NPV.

The NPV has the convenient property of being equal to the amount by which the investor increases her wealth, e.g., in the case of an automobile producing company it is the amount by which the development process increases the company's market value. As such, the strategy, which maximizes the value of the development process, is automatically the most optimal one for the developing company. The present value method shall in the following function as a reference point whenever aspects of valuation are discussed.

2.4 Models of Automotive Development

In the ensuing sections, three major models of automotive development will be introduced and compared. The emphasis here will be placed on how the models utilize prototypes to explore the design space in an uncertain environment. This is a logical extension of the previous sections, which dealt amongst other things with exploring the design space, the role of prototypes, and the uncertain and dynamic environment as a setting for the development process.

At the outset it seems sensible to introduce the various development models by the means of an analogy, which shows strong parallels to the automotive development process and its search through design space. Liker et al. (1996) present one such example: finding a meeting time for a group of employees. Three strategies for finding a feasible meeting time are available. In the first strategy the organizer starts with selecting the time and date most convenient for himself. He then starts inviting people, one at a time. The first person invited may not be able to attend at the proposed date and time and therefore bilaterally sets up a new date and time with the organizer. Then the organizer invites a second person to the meeting. However, the second person cannot make the date and time and therefore suggest a new date and time. This forces a check (feedback loop) with the other two, who may not be able to attend at the new date and time. For a larger group of employees this process may continue for a long time and involve a very large number of feedback loops before a suitable date and time is found. There is no theoretical guarantee that an optimal meeting time is found.

The second strategy tries to shorten the above-described process. Two options are available. Either the group can opt to have a meeting to decide when to have a meeting, or alternatively the organizer can opt to force the other members to show up at a given time. This second strategy generally results in a sub-optimal meeting time.

The third strategy available recognizes that the problems associated with the two first strategies result because there is a lack of information (at the group level) about feasible meeting times for each of the group members. The third strategy therefore starts out by obtaining a set of available meeting times and preferences from each of the group members to be invited. The (optimal) meeting time is then found by means of intersection between all of the members' available meeting times. This third strategy generally results in an optimal meeting time. If there is no feasible intersection then the set of meeting times would have to be expanded. This is the equivalent of the feedback loop found using the first strategy.

The search for a feasible meeting time in the above example corresponds to the search through the design space encountered during the automobile development process. The above strategies for finding an optimal meeting time each have parallels (although simplistic) to three models of automobile development. Sobek, Ward, and Liker (1999) summarize the research up to date in the automobile development process in three distinct paradigms for automobile development. These are:

1) point-based serial engineering,
2) point-based concurrent engineering, and
3) set-based concurrent engineering.

Each has its counterpart introduced with the strategies for finding a meeting time. This is summarized in Table 2.

Table 2: Analogy between the Optimal Meeting Time and the Search through Design Space

Strategies for automobile development	*Strategies for finding a meeting time*
Point-based serial engineering	Invite people one at a time
Point-based concurrent engineering	Have a meeting to find a date
Set-based concurrent engineering	Obtain set of available meeting times

Source: own creation

In the succeeding sections, each of the three strategies for automobile development will be outlined (refer in general to Sobek et al. 1999 and Liker et al. 1996).

2.4.1 Point-Based Serial Engineering

The point-based serial engineering process is the basis of much of the work done in the field of development process optimization (see, e.g., Papalambros and Wilde 1991). It resembles the generic automotive development process depicted in Figure 4. The set-up of the point-based serial engineering development process is illustrated in Figure 10.

Figure 10: Point-Based Serial Engineering

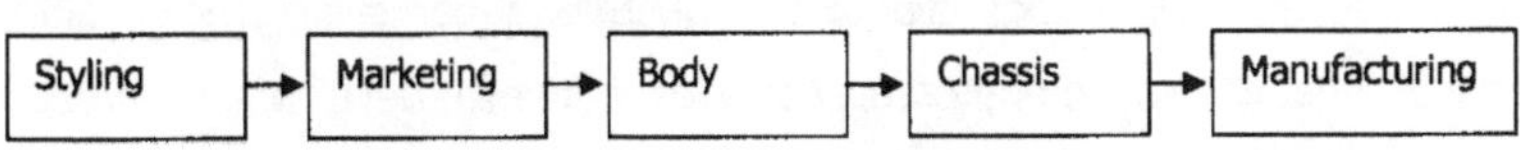

Source: Sobek et al. (1999, p. 69)

As shown the design originates in styling and then passes on in a sequential manner through marketing, body, chassis, and manufacturing. Figure 10 emphasizes how the design passes through the various functions involved in the automobile development process whereas Figure 4 illustrates the various phases, which constitute the automobile development process. Both are characterized by pronounced serial (sequential) make-up. In the process above, styling starts by conceptualizing a design based on its criteria for optimality. It then sends the design "over the wall" to marketing, which then critiques the design based on its own criteria for optimality. The design is then sent back to styling, which iterates once again and adapts the design based on the marketing function's requirements. The design then passes on to body, which also comments on the design in the same fashion as marketing. Styling once again iterates and adapts the design to body's comments. In the same manner the design passes through chassis and manufacturing.

The point-based serial engineering clearly brings to mind the first strategy for finding a meeting time (see Table 2). The strategy is characterized by a lack of information (on a pan-department level) between the participants in the development process. That is, the information set about the design is strongly segmented according to the various functions involved. When presented with a design each function goes through a design-build-test cycle based primarily on its own information set and criteria for optimality. The outcome forms the basis of a feedback loop, and the design is then updated (if needed). Each design change therefore ineludibly reduces the set of feasible design alternatives for the other participants[14]. Any decision by an upstream function could be invalidated by a change in the design by a downstream function (as was commented on above). Ward et al. (1995, p. 58) note: "Since designs are highly interconnected in obscure ways, it is generally impossible to tell whether a particular change alters decisions already made." As the interdependencies between development process participants rise so does the number of feedback loops. Because each feedback loop takes time, the result could be a lengthy problem-solving process.

It is important to notice that the point-based serial engineering strategy assumes only one "main" automotive design being developed. The feedback loops giving rise to a design change result in a changed design. However, this design is closely related to the original "main" design. Hence, this automotive development strategy is called "point-based" because only one major design at a given point in time is reviewed and

[14] The point-based development process is therefore often referred to as a "hill-climbing" process.

developed. Therefore, from a management perspective the point-based serial engineering strategy is relatively simple to manage.

2.4.2 Point-Based Concurrent Engineering

In the following sections the point-based concurrent engineering process will be presented. It is a derivative of the point-based serial engineering development process described above, and forms of the point-based concurrent engineering are currently widely implemented in the automobile industry (see Clark and Fujimoto 1991, pp. 103-104). The main objective of the point-based concurrent engineering process is to optimize the problem-solving process compared to point-based serial engineering. As remarked, the combination of interdependencies and delayed feedback loops make up the development time. In order to prevent the negative impact (in terms of development lead-time) of the delayed feedback loops the point-based concurrent engineering strategy tries to move the feedback loops forward in time. This is achieved by accentuating a parallel processing of activities (the design-build-test phases) of the various functions participating in the development process. For the current design in question, feedback from all involved functions arrives earlier. This situation is illustrated in Figure 11.

Figure 11: Point-Based Concurrent Engineering

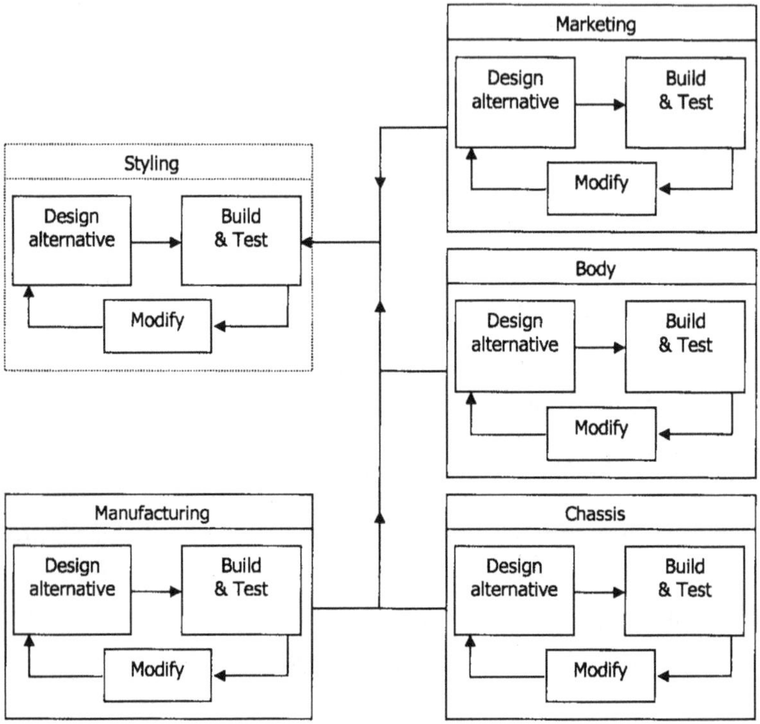

Source: own creation

In the example in Figure 11 the styling function is going through a design-build-test cycle. In doing so it simultaneously solicits an input regarding the feasibility of the design from the marketing, body, chassis, and manufacturing functions. In order to evaluate the design from styling, these functions simultaneously process the design in question in their own separate design-build-test cycles. Together the outcomes of these cycles constitute the external input into the styling function's design-build-test cycle. Naturally, the example in Figure 11 has general validity for all development functions. Each function evaluating a design would request a simultaneous (concurrent) input from the other functions.

By processing the design-build-test cycles of the various functions concurrently the negative impact (on development lead time) of segmented information is diminished. Consequently, the level of integration between the various functions in point-based concurrent engineering is greater than is the case in serial point-based engineering. This is in particular the case for the before mentioned information management process (see Figure 5). From a management perspective more attention is also required in order to manage the linkages between the functions as all participating functions are now working simultaneously. As is the case in serial point-based engineering there is only one design being investigated simultaneously. Therefore serial and concurrent point-based engineering both belong to the same (point-based) paradigm for managing the automotive development process.

2.4.3 Set-Based Concurrent Engineering

In the following sections the set-based concurrent engineering process will be presented. It is generally more extensive than the two point-based automotive development strategies and represents a fundamentally different paradigm for automotive development. The set-based strategy resembles the third strategy presented in Table 2. The set of available meeting times parallels the set of alternative designs developed in parallel using set-based concurrent engineering. In the automobile industry the set-based strategy is currently known to be implemented at Toyota (see Clark and Fujimoto 1991; Sobek 1997; and Sobek, Ward, and Liker 1999). The main objective of the set-based concurrent engineering process is to explore the design space more broadly in order to better develop an optimal design in an uncertain environment.

The theoretical construct of the design space (see Figure 6) introduced earlier represents the realm, within which the automotive development process progresses. Set-based engineering proactively explores larger areas of this design space. It starts out the development process by developing more than one design alternative in parallel. This set of design alternatives is then narrowed as time progresses, and the various automotive development phases (see Figure 4) are passed through. The set-based concurrent development strategy is illustrated in Figure 12.

Figure 12: Set-Based Concurrent Engineering (i)

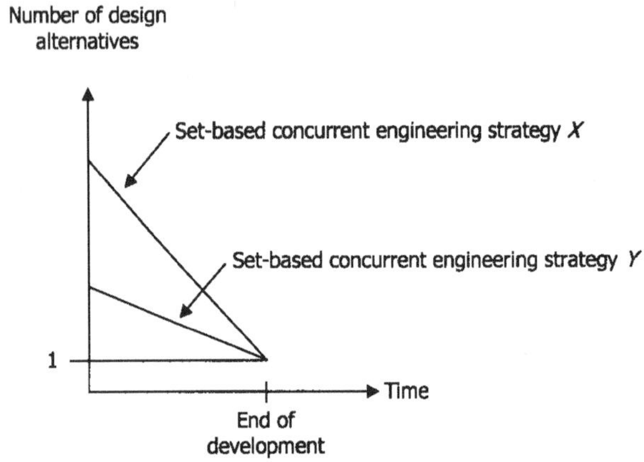

Source: own creation

Figure 12 shows two exemplary set-based concurrent development strategies: *X* and *Y*. Strategy *X* explores the design space to a greater extent than does strategy *Y*, as strategy *X* starts out at a higher intersection on the ordinate. As time progresses and the various development phases are gone through the suboptimal design alternatives are terminated. This leads to the negative slope of straight line representing the strategies *X* and *Y*. The horizontal line starting at 1 on the ordinate may be thought of as the point-based concurrent engineering strategy. An equivalent manner of representing the set-based concurrent development strategy is shown in Figure 13.

Figure 13: Set-Based Concurrent Engineering (ii)

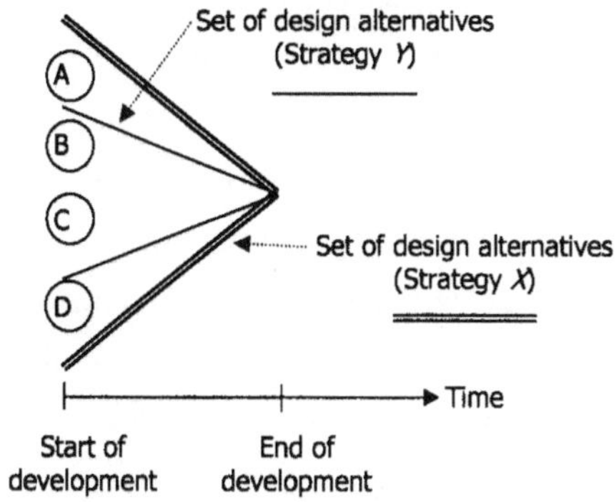

Source: own creation

Figure 13 also shows the two set-based concurrent development strategies *X* and *Y*. Strategy *Y* explores some of the design space with the design alternatives *B* and *C*. In comparison, Strategy *X* explores more of the design space with the design alternatives *A* and *D* in addition to *B* and *C*. As time passes, the set of alternatives developed in parallel is reduced until only one design alternative is left. The mechanism for reducing the set is based on a set of criteria, which in turn is based on the dual objectives of accomplishing a high degree of external and internal integrity. As the set of design alternatives is reduced by management, the development process ultimately converges on one final design alternative (in Figure 13: either *A*, *B*, *C*, or *D*), which is then implemented.

From a technical perspective the selected set of design alternatives at the start of development is often characterized by a greater degree of similarities. The designs chosen for development (e.g., designs *A*, *B*, *C*, and *D* in figure Figure 13) share common traits. I.e., the designs share one or more technical details. In this manner management can investigate the trade-offs between various design specifications. The purpose behind this approach is to be able to explore systematically the areas of the design space (see Figure 6), which management believes to have the greatest potential for finding an optimal design. A given design may well be optimal in one scenario even though it is non-optimal in another scenario. By developing design alternatives for different scenarios management has the flexibility to await the resolution of uncertainty and then at the end of development choose the best design for implementation.

In practice any automobile development process employing the set-based concurrent strategy would be faced with several challenges. The management of simultaneously developing several designs in parallel poses a significant challenge for the developing organization. [15] Compared to the first two development strategies, the set-based strategy in effect multiplies the effort needed to manage the automobile development process. There is a higher degree of invested resources and associated managerial resources needed to manage the development effort. The set-based strategy also tends to be more expensive than a point-based development strategy. The broader exploration of the design space must therefore add up to higher expected cash flows in order to offset the higher degree of invested resources before an automotive company would employ this type of process to develop its cars.

Based on their research of the product development process Wheelwright and Clark (1992) utilize a similar framework as Sobek, Ward, and Liker (1999). Wheelwright and Clark introduce the "development funnel" as a framework for managing a set of design alternatives during the development process. This is illustrated in Figure 14.

[15] Set-based development requires specific capabilities and assets, which support such a development process. This aspect will be discussed comprehensively in chapter 3.

Figure 14: The Development Funnel

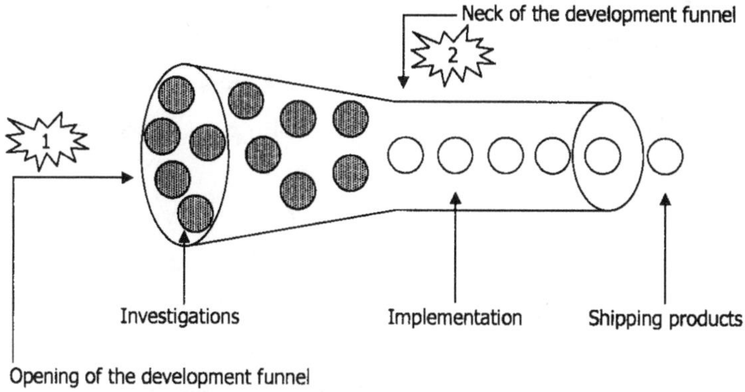

Source: adapted from Clark and Wheelwright (1992, p. 112)

The shaded circles represent the design alternatives currently being investigated by the automobile company. As time passes, the suboptimal alternatives are no longer investigated. This is seen by the narrowing of the funnel. Finally one design alternative is selected and subsequently implemented. At the end of product development the design alternative is typically mass produced and shipped to customers. Figure 14 is in principle equivalent to Figure 13. Both utilize the concept of working with sets of alternatives in parallel.

In reality, the actual development funnel observed through empirical research is not as smooth and straightforward is conceptualized in Figure 14. Wheelwright and Clark (1992) identify a great variety of development funnels in their empirical research. E.g., some funnels consist of several separate funnels, which only at a later point in time converge. In this work though, the primary focus shall be first and foremost on establishing general concepts for the automotive development process. For this purpose the above generalization of set-based development shall suffice.

Apart from the (natural) variations in various applied development strategies, Wheelwright and Clark (1992) generalize their fieldwork concerning the development funnel and identify two main challenges on the subject of managing the funnel in practice. The first challenge for management deals with the opening the development funnel (labelled by the "1" in Figure 14). The second challenge deals with the process of narrowing the funnel and selecting the final design for implementation at the neck of the funnel (labelled by the "2" in Figure 14). I.e., the first challenge occurs at the beginning of the development process, and the second challenge takes place between "1" and "2" in Figure 14.

As was mentioned in chapter 2.2 the search process is fraught with uncertainty. In principal it is possible to classify three sources of uncertainty regarding the automobile development effort. From a valuation perspective, the first two uncertainties exist primarily when one takes a neoclassic approach to finance. It is this approach, which is chosen for this work (see the delimitation in chapter 1). In the context of the automobile development process, the central assumption is one of no behavioural uncertainty arising as a result of informational asymmetry between the participants in the development process. For instance this is the case when a standard option valuation formula is applied to a real asset. The two first sources of uncertainty can be viewed as a starting point to the majority of the valuation models currently existing in financial economics (Merton and Bodie 2005). The third source of uncertainty arises when one makes the assumption of behavioural uncertainty arising due to asymmetric information (see, e.g., Barbaris and Thaler 2003 for an overview). Uncertainties of this kind arise in almost any type of cooperative arrangement. Therefore, the third source also applies to the automotive development process. In practice both the neoclassic and behavioural uncertainty approaches will likely be of relevance and therefore complement each other (Merton and Bodie 2005, p. 6).

In the following the three sources of uncertainties are briefly outlined:

1) First, there is technical uncertainty because it is often not certain beforehand what will be the outcome of the design-build-test cycle. This uncertainty is associated with the objective of achieving a high degree of internal integrity in the automobile.

2) Second, there is market uncertainty, and it can be linked to the objective of achieving a high degree of external integrity in the automobile.[16] Specifically for the purposes of this thesis, the information set (vector) shall be viewed as a function of time and the two sources of uncertainty (technical and market).[17] The actual revelation of the market and technical uncertainties determines the optimality of a given design alternative. E.g., a result of a design-build-test cycle could be a technical failure. This is equivalent to ending up in a "worst case" scenario, which was probably not known with certainty from the outset of the project. The evolutionary path taken by a given project depends on the two uncertainties and is not known in advance.

3) Third, there is behavioural uncertainty arising from the mentioned information asymmetries. Compared to the equilibrium results prescribed by neoclassic theory, behavioural uncertainty leads to certain inefficiencies compared to best case with no information asymmetry (Merton and Bodie 2005, p. 5).

The objectives of high internal and external integrity are interlinked. Integrity is also interlinked with the two other performance benchmarks (time and productivity) for the automotive development process (see Figure 3). Therefore, any discussion of handling the two challenges of the development funnel is interlinked with the three objectives of the development process:

1) The first challenge for management is to open up the development funnel. The objective herewith is to cope with uncertainty. The optimality of a design alternative depends on its contribution to internal and external integrity. As this contribution is not certain in advance, management can opt to explore the design space more fully (as already discussed). Therefore if one design alternative fails then management has the option to continue developing another alternative. This flexibility is extremely important. The design-build-test cycle(s) represent a learning process whereupon the information

[16] Market uncertainty and technical uncertainty play a very important role in this thesis. They will both be discussed comprehensively in subsequent chapters.

[17] Note that the variable uncertainty is in this thesis primarily understood as the second moment of a probability distribution.

asset (vector) is augmented. Combining the flexibility to adapt the development strategy according to the unfolding of this information helps management reduce the impact of negative information in addition to taking advantage of positive information.

2) The second challenge of the development funnel is to narrow its neck until the process converges and one design alternative is left, which is then implemented. This narrowing process implies an active involvement of management in "killing" non-optimal alternatives (Waites 2002, p. 19). As Clark and Fujimoto (1991, p. 113) state: this is the "hard part", and it is difficult to quantify (Quinn 1986, p. 19). In thinning the alternatives management must rely on a set of criteria to guide in making these decisions. Due to the complexity of the automobile (see Figure 2), the symbiotic relationship between integrity, time, and productivity (see Figure 3), and the uncertainties (technical and market), it is a formidable challenge to develop this set of criteria, which give specific and sensible advice. The following analyses will deal actively with modelling these criteria within a capital markets-oriented framework.

There is a trade-off involved with both opening up the funnel and subsequently narrowing it based on the unfolding of information. The more the funnel is opened, the more management must later thin out the alternatives that are not attractive. If the funnel is not opened sufficiently then management has limited options afterward and must continue with alternatives that are not as attractive. Conversely, by developing more than one design alternative simultaneously management must invest a greater degree of resources in the automotive development. This trade-off will be dealt with in particular in the subsequent chapters.

A principal assumption of the set-based concurrent development strategy is that the set of designs being developed are interchangeable. E.g., if one design fails then management has the flexibility (option) to continue developing one or more of the other designs as these also belong to the feasible set of designs. This principle has a twofold significance. First, at the level of the complete automobile each design alternative represents a feasible design for mass production. Second, at the level of the automotive subsystems this principle means that each of the subsystem designs represent a feasible subsystem design alternative. This aspect is illustrated in Figure 15.

Figure 15: Modularity and Set-Based Concurrent Engineering

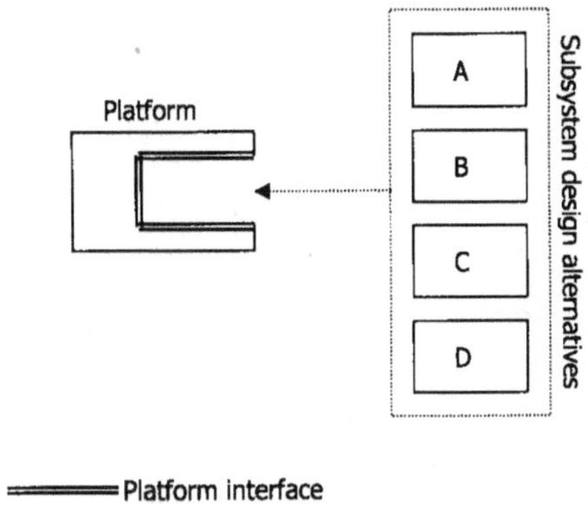

Source: own creation

Figure 15 illustrates the example of interchangeable alternative subsystem designs *A*, *B*, *C*, and *D*. Each of these fits into the slot in the platform (the automobile). That is, each of the designs can be characterized as a module with an interface that matches the platform interface. In the case of the automobile these interfaces could be component specifications (such as height, weight, material, etc.), performance characteristics (such as heat resistance, durability, etc.), and subjective perceptions (such as acceptable noise level, smell, design, etc.).

The platform interface (in Figure 15) equates design standards, which all modules that interact with other automotive subsystems must adhere to. In fact Baldwin and Clark (1997) and Baldwin and Clark (2002) list certain characteristics of a modular design. At the heart of their reasoning is a segmentation of the design information set in two types: visible and hidden information. The subsystem specifications, which deal with the subsystem's interactions with other parts of the automobile, is the visible design information. It relates to the design standards, and in order for modularity to work, it should be "precise, unambiguous, and complete" (Baldwin and Clark 1997, p. 86).

Baldwin and Clark (1997) further list three categories of visible information (see Table 3).

Table 3: Three Categories of Visible Design Information

Visible design information		
1. Architecture	2. Interfaces	3. Standards
Specifies what subsystems will be part of the system and what their functions will be	Detailed descriptions of how the subsystems will interact (how they fit together, connect, and communicate)	Detailed descriptions for testing a subsystem's conformity to the design rules and for measuring the modules performance

Source: Own creation, adapted from Baldwin and Clark (1997, p. 86)

A requirement for a modular design is that management invests in creating the visible design information (see Table 3). This is a time consuming and costly process. Furthermore, by settling on a certain set of visible information management markedly determines the advantages (or disadvantages) of a modular design.

The subsystem specifications, which do not interact with other parts of the automobile, is the hidden information. This design information deals with the internal workings of the subsystem and does not affect the design beyond the local subsystem. In this way the entire set of automotive design information is not communicated during the design-build-test cycles to the other departments. Only the visible design information is passed on, and this leads to a simplification in the amount of information communicated. As long as the automotive design lies within the design standards, management has the flexibility to choose between the alternative designs, which are being developed concurrently.

The above outline of the set-based concurrent development strategy and the implicit assumption of modularity lead to the following portrayal of the set-based development strategy.

Figure 16: Toyota's Parallel Set-Narrowing Process

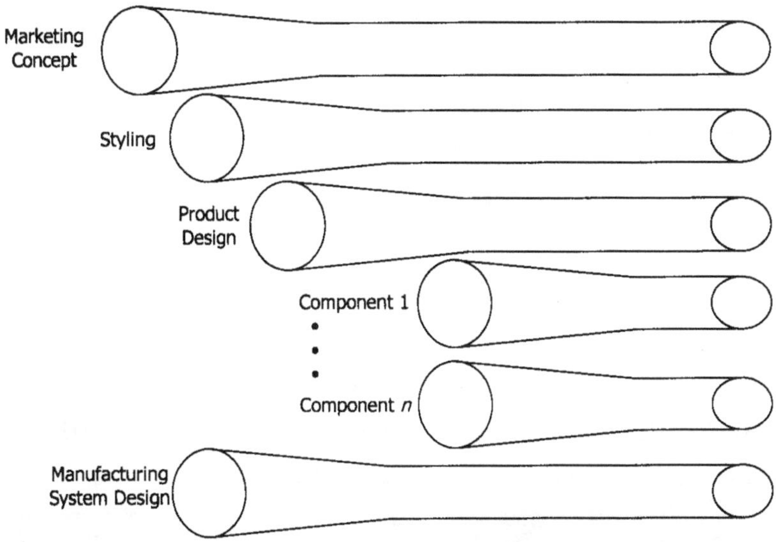

Source: own creation and based on a sketch by Toyota's general manager of body engineering in 1993, see Ward et al. (1995, p. 49)

Figure 16 shows the development process currently in use by Toyota as reported by Ward et al. (1995). Toyota's development process shows a strong degree of developing alternative designs concurrently (compare to Figure 15) on a subsystems level. The development phases of the various departments in Figure 16 (Marketing, Styling, Product Engineering, and Manufacturing / Process Engineering) are slightly sequential. This compares to the "Flexible Model" (Figure 17) of development investigated by Iansiti (1995) based on empirical research primarily in the computer industry.

Figure 17: The Flexible Model of Development

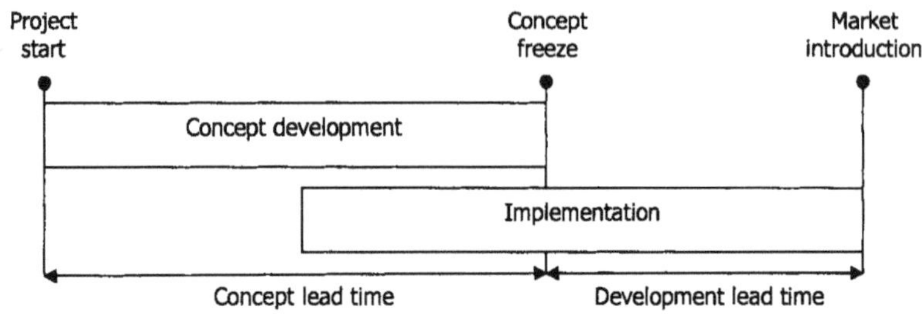

Source: adapted from Iansiti (1995, p. 40)

Iansiti (1995) observed that well-performing companies applied development processes with an implementation phase, which starts as early as possible. In Figure 17 this corresponds to the slightly sequential setup of the concept development and implementation phases. The flexible model can thus be seen as a refinement of the concurrent development process with a focus on overlapping concept development and implementation stages. Transferred to Figure 16 this insight corresponds to the concurrent narrowing of the various funnels. E.g., manufacturing has started its implementation before some of the component designs have been developed completely.

2.5 Comparative Analysis of the Point- and Set-Based Models of Development

In the following the point- and set-based models of automotive development will be compared. The purpose is to analyze how each of these models shapes the managerial decision-making process. This is done in terms of their impact on flexibility, uncertainty, and the investments costs required. Table 4 illustrates the setup for the comparison.

Table 4: Comparison of Point- and Set-Based Development

Development strategy	*Point-based*	*Set-based*
Number of design alternatives	1	>1
Level of integration needed	low	high
Cost of strategy	(+)	(-)
Uncertainty	(-)	(+)
Flexibility	(-)	(+)

(+) = advantage
(-) = disadvantage
Source: Own creation

The above table compares the point- and set-based strategies along several dimensions. Both are concerned with developing an automobile, but accomplish this objective in very different ways. The point-based strategy emphasizes "doing it right the first time" (Ward et al. 1995, p. 48). Given the information set at the beginning of the development process management should focus all their resources on the current most optimal design. The set-based strategy alternatively recognizes that are currently several design ideas available next to the current most optimal design. With the aim of exploring the design space more fully the set-based strategy starts out the development process with more than one design alternative being developed in parallel.

2.5.1 Level of Integration

The factor "Level of integration needed" in Table 4 refers to the firm-specific capabilities necessary for the implementation of either a point- or set-based development strategy. Compared to a point-based strategy, a set-based strategy is more difficult to implement, and is characterized by a "high" level of integration. Due to the multitude of projects developed in parallel management must not only watch one project closely but several projects simultaneously. Moreover there are most likely several interactions between the design alternatives being developed, further complicating the effort. That is, there is likely a correlation matrix indifferent from 0 between the various design alternatives. Chapter 3 shall deal extensively with the aspects of capabilities relating to the automotive development process. Chapters 4 and 5 shall deal with the intraproject correlation(s) in terms of a valuation model.

2.5.2 Cost of Strategy

As clarified previously, one apparent difference between the two development strategies lies in the required investment costs. This is the factor "cost of strategy" in Table 4. The set-based strategy basically has two investment components. The first is a result of the parallel development of more than one alternative. The required investment is proportionately higher than is the case in point-based development. The second investment component is an upfront investment cost, which is required to set up the visible design information (see Table 3). In other words, the automotive platform must be developed in order to support the design alternatives. This makes exploring the design space more fully utilizing a set-based approach a costly proposition. The higher investment costs seemingly make the set-based development process very inefficient due to the fact that several costly alternatives are developed, but in the end only one is implemented. This is likely a reason why the wide majority of automotive firms currently employ forms of the point-based development process.

2.5.3 Uncertainty and Flexibility

The relevance of the final two variables "uncertainty" and "flexibility" in Table 4 depends to a great degree on the chosen development strategy. [18] As stated previously uncertainty typifies the development process due to the evolution of the information set (see, e.g., Figure 5). It is this probability-weighted spread of possible outcomes, which makes the actual outcomes of the development process likely to differ from the expected outcomes. If there is only one design alternative in the pipeline then management must stay with the outcome of the design-build-test cycle(s). This is the case with the point-based development strategy. In this circumstance management has

[18] In subsequent chapters it will be contended that it is the automotive development characteristics of uncertainty and flexibility, which are key value drivers capable of explaining and optimizing the development process.

no flexibility to choose a different design alternative, because it has developed only one. A different situation results when the set-based development process is employed. At the end of the development phase there is one outcome available per developed design alternative.[19] Management now has the flexibility to choose between the various designs and implementing the most valuable design. If one design alternative turns out poorly then management does not have to stay with that alternative but can switch to a better design alternative. The positive advantage of having the flexibility to choose the maximum value of more than one design alternative also depends on the level of correlation between the design alternatives. I.e., the correlation matrix plays a crucial rule in elucidating what evolutionary paths the individual alternatives could take. It remains to be modelled how managerial flexibility in the set-based strategy impacts the value of the development process when the individual design alternatives are uncertain and mutually correlated.

2.5.4 Trade-off between Investment Costs and Flexibility to Switch

Based on the comparisons above there is an important trade-off between the point- and set-based development strategies. The set-based strategy gives management the flexibility to switch (or equivalently choose) between the various developed designs, but the set-based strategy is also most likely to be the most resource demanding development strategy.[20] In order to have this flexibility to choose, management actively builds in flexibility into the development process by utilizing a set-based setup. As clarified this comes at a higher investment cost, though. The trade-off is illustrated in Figure 18.

[19] The actual outcomes depend on the evolution of the technical and market uncertainties for each design alternative.

[20] This is a difficult trade-off to solve and requires a more formal framework, which is capable of illustrating it. The framework is developed in chapter 4 and put to use in chapter 5.

Figure 18: Trade-off between Investment Costs and Flexibility to Switch

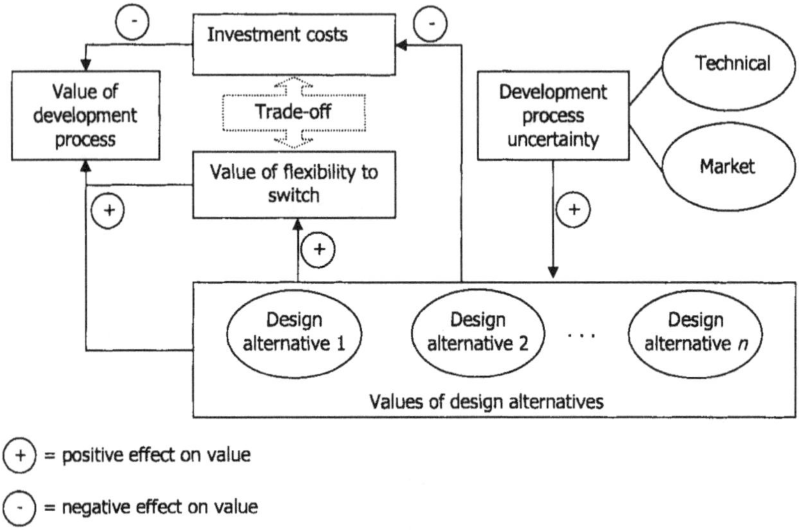

Source: own creation

The objective for management is to maximize the value of the development process (the far left part of Figure 18). Figure 18 shows the technical and market uncertainties driving the values of the individual design alternatives, which in turn represent central components of the automotive development process value. This perspective of value creation would also be included in, e.g., a PV calculation. In addition, the uncertainties surrounding the value of the respective design alternatives also drive the value of the flexibility to choose (switch) between the alternative design alternatives 1 through *n*. This aspect of automotive development process value creation would not be part of a customary valuation of the automotive development process. The value of the flexibility to switch positively influences the value of the development process. But then again, a higher number of designs developed in parallel also results in higher investment costs (a negative influence). This is the "trade-off" in Figure 18. In other words, management has to start out the development process by deciding on a number of design alternatives to develop in parallel, ranging from 1 to a potential of *n* alternatives. This exactly recapitulates the hitherto outline of the point-based and set-based paradigms for automobile development. The point-based strategy basically develops one design alternative whereas the set-based develops more than one design alternative concurrently. If one is willing to reduce the discussion about the automobile development process to the number of design alternatives then Figure 18 serves as a figurative starting point for a subsequent valuation model of the automotive development process. This valuation model will be presented in chapter 4. To summarize it is helpful to state Figure 18 in terms of an equation. This leads to the following breakdown of the value of the automobile development process:

(2.2) $$\text{ENPV} = -I_0 + \text{PV}(\text{FCF}) + \text{Value of flexibility}$$

where

ENPV = Extended Net Present Value

I_0 = Present value of expected investment outlays

Figure 18 illustrates that flexibility in an uncertain development environment has a positive value, but this flexibility comes at a price. The choice facing management is therefore how much flexibility to build into the automotive development process given the increasing investment costs of doing so. What drives the value of this flexibility is the amount and correlations of the uncertainties underlying the development process. Therefore the above-mentioned trade-off can be rephrased as a trade-off between the technical and market uncertainties and the investment costs of the automobile development process.

It is the framework for the automobile development process presented in this chapter, which shall be utilized in the following chapters to conduct a more extensive analysis of the automobile development process. As alluded to earlier the purpose of this analysis is eventually to present a quantitative valuation model of the automobile development process, which is capable of valuing the indicated interdependencies.

2.6 Chapter Summary

This chapter dealt with the automobile, the structure and function of automotive development, and three different ways of developing an automobile. Categorized as a product, the automobile can be characterized by high degrees of product complexity both internally and externally. The challenge for the developing company is to develop the automobile in a timely manner while achieving high levels of productivity and integrity.

A key result concerning the automotive development process is the role of information about the technical and market prospects of the automobile. The focus on the physical product as such becomes secondary to the information resulting from the unfolding uncertainties surrounding the development effort. An essential element in generating information about the uncertainties is the exploration of the design space through well directed design-build-test cycles employing prototypes as information generating vehicles. Consequently management should place their emphasis on the way prototypes of design alternatives are employed in order to explore the design space.

Chapter 2.3 presented three models of automotive development, which were introduced by means of an example: finding an optimal meeting time. The simplest development model is point-based serial engineering. According to this model management chooses the current most optimal design and develops it through several sequential iterative cycles. The second model is point-based concurrent engineering. It also chooses the current most optimal design for development. However, it is developed employing concurrent feedback cycles from all participating development functions and as such presents a logical optimization of the serial development process. The third and final development model is set-based concurrent engineering. The differences to point-based concurrent engineering consist in the size of the set of design alternatives developed in parallel and the implicit notion of a modular product architecture. The concept of a development funnel was applied to illustrate the managerial effects of set-based development. It was shown that there are two main managerial implications pertaining to managing the development funnel: opening the mouth of the funnel and killing non-optimal design alternatives. Finally, in chapter 2.4 the point- and set-based models of concurrent engineering were compared according to their performance on the important dimensions of: exploration of the design space, level of integration, investment costs, accommodation of uncertainty, and managerial flexibilities provided. Based on these performance criteria, a trade-off was identified between a more extensive exploration of the design space and the higher investment costs associated with developing more than one design alternative in parallel. This trade-off is modelled explicitly in chapter 4, and chapter 5 presents numerical examples of how to determine an optimal size of the set of design alternatives to develop in parallel.

Chapter 3: Competitive Advantage and the Automotive Development Process

The purpose of this chapter is to deal mainly with answering subproblem 2 of the problem statement:
What role does the automotive development process play in helping the developing company attain a sustainable competitive advantage in the marketplace?

The overall purpose of this chapter is to analyse how firm-level efficiency advantages help develop superior automobiles. In doing so, the automobile development process is placed in the context of the strategic management literature. The essential building blocks for the analysis of efficiency advantages are first introduced and explained. The analysis, which follows, can be considered an extension of the outline of the automobile development process in chapter 2. It draws on the models of strategic management as well as various empirical findings from the automobile industry in order to present a strategic management analysis of the automobile development process.

As was the case with the previous chapter the findings presented here serve as an underlying framework for the analyses in the coming chapters where the automotive development process is analyzed from the viewpoint of the automotive company's owners in terms of a quantitative valuation model. That is, the focus in the latter part of the thesis will ultimately be on the cash flows, which result from a given set of actions. In other words, this chapter serves as a preliminary study of the automotive development process based on the methodology employed in the strategic management literature.

The outline for the current chapter is as follows. The first part of this chapter starts with briefly explaining the objective of strategic management as to achieve a sustainable competitive advantage in the market. The emphasis here is particularly on presenting the framework employed in the resource-based view (RBV) of the corporation as it pertains to firm-level efficiency advantages. The second part of this chapter utilizes the strategic management framework and links it to empirical research of the automotive development process. This allows a breakdown of an otherwise very complex process into key components, which drive value for the developing company. The third section of this chapter focuses on Toyota's development system and classifies it within a strategic management framework. Toyota represents one of the major automobile developers worldwide, and its automobile development system yields several insights into successful development systems.

3.1 Achieving a Competitive Advantage Utilizing the Development Process

The strategic objective of the corporation is to achieve a sustainable[21] competitive advantage in the market (refer in general to Rumelt, Schendel, and Teece 1991). A competitive advantage is always identified relative to the competition in a given market segment. I.e., when a given company is superior to other competitors it succeeds in generally being able to supply its customers with a product and/or service, which the competition cannot do as competently. Strategic management can therefore be rephrased as the process of creating market imperfections. In other words, a sustainable competitive advantage manifests itself in the ability to generate economic rents in the long term.[22] Superiority is measured in terms of how well the company meets the critical success factors (CSF). Among the multitude of buying criteria for customers in a given market segment, the CSF are the most important buying criteria

---

[21] Sustainability is understood here as referring to the long term effects of strategy. I.e. a sustainable advantage is a durable advantage.

[22] Shapiro (1991) defines rents as the ability to consistently earn returns that exceed the opportunity cost of capital. In the long run, rents are more often observed in the real markets (such as e.g. for automobiles) than in the financial markets. The degree of market perfection thus is decisive to determining the degree of rents achievable. These in turn (in an efficient market) are reflected in the market price of the company's equity.

for the customer, such as, e.g.: price, reliability, functionality, aesthetics, image, etc. (see Hall 1993). Further, a sustainable competitive advantage for companies can be defined as the case when they "consistently produce products with attributes which correspond to the key buying criteria for the majority of the customers in their targeted market." (Hall 1993, p. 610).

3.1.1 The Organizational Process of Sequential Choice

Mintzberg (1978) refers to strategy as an organizational process of sequential choice regarding resource deployment. Strategy therefore implies that management aspires to meet the CSFs better than the competition by investing the endowed resources in successive stages. The factor time therefore plays a crucial role in connection with the management of resources. Management does not make all the decisions at time t_0, effectively fixing the strategy, and then in time passively adheres to the original plan. Rather, management has the flexibility to make investment decisions in time and thereby actively seek out the best opportunities for resource deployment, potentially deviating from the original plan.[23]

Recommendations for managing the above process of investing resources sequentially are the subject of various models in the strategic management literature. The models presented here give recommendations to corporate management about value-creating avenues of venture. There are two major groups of strategic management models. The first group concentrates on the external environment of the corporation whereas the second group concentrates on the internal environment of the corporation. Historically strategic management research started with an emphasis on the first group of models. The second group has recently been at the center of much research. In order to facilitate the process of reading it is meaningful to briefly elaborate on the models and

[23] The amount of uncertainty present in a given project determines the difference between making all the decisions at time t_0 and alternatively making decisions in time. If there is no uncertainty, there is no difference between the two alternatives. Uncertainty and making decisions flexibly economically translate into a positive option value. This point is of great interest in latter parts of the thesis.

their central concepts and definitions as they are applied within this work. The following sections shall be devoted to this purpose.

3.1.2 Industry Structural Analysis

In the 1960s the Boston Consulting Group developed a model (the growth matrix), which linked the growth of a market to the firm's relative market share. The focus here is primarily on the external environment of the corporation. Then in the 1970s and 1980s the models of industry structural analysis were developed. The focus here is also primarily on the external environment of the corporation and how a corporation should invest its resources in the context of a specific market constellation. A prime proponent of this view is Porter (1980) in his seminal work "Competitive strategy". Shapiro (1989) enhances this view of strategic management with a dynamic modelling [24] of the competitive forces in the industry. The external models of management strategy share the view that rents are achieved through privileged market positions. Often the external view of the corporation is mentioned in literature as trying to achieve a strategic "fit". I.e., management matches its resources to identified white spaces in the market, and the key to competitive advantage lies in where the company chooses to compete (e.g., Stalk, Philip, and Shulman 1992; and Johnson and Scholes 2002).

3.1.3 Resources and Capabilities

The second group of models focuses on the assets available to a corporation and its use of these in key business processes. This approach will be referred to here as the RBV[25], and its emphasis is on the internal environment of the corporation. The RBV "emphasizes building competitive advantage through capturing entrepreneurial rents stemming from fundamental firm-level efficiency advantages." (Teece, Pisano, and Shuen 1997, p. 510). This indicates that competitive advantage (rents) is achieved

---

[24] Analogous to the dynamic programming approach known from decision-making theory.

[25] Teece, Pisano, and Shuen (1997) further discern this approach from the capabilities based approach. In this work the approach taken by Peteraf (1993, p. 179) shall be applied. The term "resource-based" shall therefore semantically encompass both the assets and capabilities of a corporation.

through mastery of both corporate assets and business processes if "they are matched appropriately to environmental opportunities" (Peteraf 1993, p. 179). Often this focus on the internal environment of the corporation is referred to in the literature as trying to achieve a strategic "stretch". According to this view management should not only exploit existing resources and business processes in current markets but should also aim to develop (stretch) its resource base (assets and businesses processes) and apply it to new markets. I.e., the key to competitive advantage lies in how the company chooses to compete.

Both the concepts of industry structural analysis and the RBV play a potentially important role in understanding and optimizing the automobile development process. However, the automobile development process, as it has been presented in chapter 2, concerns first and foremost the business process of identifying an existing market need (or a need yet to be created by the company) and subsequently utilizing the corporate resource base to try to fulfil that need. This places the automobile development process squarely in the field of the RBV of corporate strategy. Although the RBV is of great importance Kogut and Kulatilaka (1994) exploit both industry structural analysis and the RBV in their work and suggest to "bridge these two streams of thought" (Kogut and Kulatilaka 1994, p. 53) for the purpose of evaluating corporate resource investments. Equivalently Peteraf and Barney (2003, p. 312) state: "RBT [Resource-based theory] is not a substitute for industry-level analytic tools, such as 5-forces analysis (Porter, 1980) and game theory. It is not a substitute for strategic group analysis or for analysis of the macro environment. Rather, it is a complement to these tools." An equivalent approach shall be put to use in latter parts of the thesis, in particular when attending to the previously mentioned valuation model of the automobile development process. For now, the RBV shall be dealt with in detail in the following.

As introduced above the RBV employs two central terms in explaining how the corporation can attain a competitive advantage in the market: These are "resources" and "capabilities". It is through a simultaneous optimization of the corporation's resources and capabilities that management can achieve a competitive advantage in the market. Pandza et al. (2003, p. 1013) define resources as "assets that a firm owns or has access to." Resources can be tangible (e.g., Chandy and Tellis 1998) and intangible (e.g., Henderson and Clark 1990) and represent "more or less a firm-specific asset to which a monetary value can be attached" (Pandza et al. 2003, p. 1013). Teece, Pisano, and Shuen (1997) give some examples of resources such as technology, finances, reputation, institutional settings, organizational boundaries[26], and Hall (1993) alludes to the importance of the organizational culture as an important asset. The second component of the RBV is capabilities. Stalk, Philip, and Shulman (1992, p. 60) define capabilities as "a set of business processes strategically understood." A similar definition is given by Tallman and Fladmoe-Lindquist (2002, pp. 118-119): "capabilities go beyond the realm of pure knowledge to include the broader set actions and structures that are critical to competitive advantage." Within the set of corporate business processes, capabilities are the processes that are critical for the corporation's aspiration to attain a sustainable competitive advantage. Kogut and Kulatilaka (1994, p. 61) give examples of capabilities such as "creating quality, being more flexible, and responding to the market quickly." There is therefore a clear connection between organizational resources and capabilities: Resources are the building blocks for capabilities.[27]

Pandza et al. (2003, p. 1011) note that both resources and capabilities "have characteristics that make them difficult to trade or imitate; hence performance differences between firms are to be expected, as they are a natural outcome of the idiosyncratic and path dependent histories in which resources and capabilities have evolved." The quote touches upon a quintessential tenet of the RBV of corporate strategy. A corporation with a competitive advantage cannot easily be imitated by the competition due to the uniqueness of its resource base (resources and capabilities) since the resource base is a result of an idiosyncratic business process. The two

[26] E.g. the degree of integration (vertical and horizontal) with the environment.

[27] From a valuation perspective there is an interesting parallel to organizational capabilities. In order to value an organizational capability one needs to span the vector of payoffs stemming from the capability with marketed asset prices. This is the well-known duplication principle, e.g., as applied in option pricing. This is an important point, which shall be discussed in the latter part of the thesis.

interdependent aspects at the core of this uniqueness of the corporation are irreversibility and duplication.[28] Irreversibility results from an inability or unwillingness to change a current organizational and technical investment in the resource base. This is the well-known concept of inertia from organizational theory. This means that at least in the short run the corporate resource base is "sticky" to some degree.[29] Teece, Pisano, and Shuen (1997, p. 514) see the explanation for this phenomenon partly in the lack of time and suitable assets needed for change and further state that "business development is... an extremely complex process." The second aspect of corporate uniqueness is caused by the difficulty of duplicating a given asset and capability structure. The competitive advantage is thus derived from a unique sequence of decisions regarding resource deployment, which the competition can neither duplicate for lack of the assets, the needed capabilities, or time. Pandza et al. (2003, p. 1012) further state that duplication is made difficult due to: "the complex, ambiguous and even paradoxical nature of organisational phenomenon." In other words, causal ambiguity (e.g., Collis 1994), the multitude of variables ultimately determining corporate performance, and managers with bounded rationality conjointly affect the durability of the competitive advantage and consequently the dissipation of rents.

The uniqueness of the corporate resource base has in effect created a market imperfection. A great deal of research within the RBV is focused on generating prescriptions for an optimal sequential decision-making process in order to create these imperfections. Though, recognizing that the organization not only should optimize its path, but it is also constrained by it, makes it urgent to analyze the effect of compounding in the decision-making process.[30] The net effect of the path-dependent business process is an asymmetrical payoff structure, which is unique to the corporation. Because these asymmetrical payoff structures are known to be potentially

[28] The terms "irreversibility" and "duplication" are chosen here due to their parallel use in option pricing, which will play an important role later in this work.

[29] Bowman and Hurry (1993, p. 766) discuss organizational inertia in terms of real options.

[30] Indeed there is a strong parallel to the analysis of compound options known from financial economics.

very valuable for the corporation[31] the following sections shall explore in more detail the specific nature of capabilities.

3.1.4 Meta-Learning and Absorptive Capacity

A basis for a more dynamic view of capabilities is provided by Tallman and Fladmoe-Lindquist (2002, p. 120), who refer to capabilities as: "complex knowledge resources," thereby linking organizational information with organizational capabilities. As has been previously discussed the set of information ex ante is most likely to be unlike the set of information available to the organization ex post (e.g., Pandza et al. 2003).[32] This is due to the existence of market and technical uncertainty. I.e., the organization is situated in an external (related to market uncertainty) and internal (related to technical uncertainty) environment, which changes with time. This changing information functions as a primary input to the managerial decision-making process. In other words, the organization learns from the updating of the information set. This is the so-called single-loop learning (Argyris 1983; and Lei, Hitt, and Bettis 1996), which is focused on influencing behavioural outcomes. A key ingredient of organizational capabilities is therefore how an organization learns from and utilizes the changing information set. Here organizational flexibility plays an important role. Bryan (2002, p. 20) notes: "The strategic idea is constantly to adapt the corporation to this fluid environment." The degree to which the organization is capable of exercising its flexibility is termed a firm's "absorptive capacity" by Cohen and Levinthal (1990). They state that "the ability of a firm to recognize the value of new... information, assimilate it, and apply it to commercial ends is critical to its innovative capabilities." (Cohen and Levinthal 1990, p. 128). By exercising its flexibility management is actually stretching the organizational

---

[31] Options also have asymmetrical payoff structures and represent leveraged financial instruments with a potentially very valuable payoff.

[32] In financial economics the updating of the vector of relevant information about the market value of an asset is linked to the volatility of asset returns. Likewise, the volatility of firm-specific value drivers can be linked to the updating of the information vector.

resource base. This process is itself a capability, making clear the interrelationship between information and organizational capabilities.

Several successful companies are very mindful of the role of information in their organization. Faulkner (1996, p. 55) notes that: "The Japanese process is often described as a rapid series of market probes, with product design changes being driven by the learning obtained from these probes." The purpose of these firms' investments is to gain valuable information about project opportunities as time progresses. Correspondingly Bernardo and Chowdhry (2001, p. 212) note: "when making investment decisions, firms will optimally consider both the stand-alone cash flows and the value of the information they expect to learn." Likewise Nonaka (1990, p. 28) refers to Japanese organizations as utilizing an "'information creating' model." I.e., management consciously partakes in making a continuous stream of relatively small investments in order to learn. Based on research from the computer industry Iansiti (1995, p. 56) makes a similar observation: "The development process proactively inquired into the uncertainties that characterize technology and market". He further quotes the CEO of one of the participating companies as having said: "The source of our competitiveness in this industry is our ability to manage in a chaotic environment. But it's more proactive than that. We actually help create the chaos in the first place – that's what keeps a lot of potential competitors out." (Iansiti 1995, p. 56).

A more advanced type of organizational learning occurs when an organization utilizes so-called "double-loop" learning (also known as meta-learning) processes aimed at creating "new insight, heuristics and a collective consciousness within the organization." (Lei, Hitt, and Bettis 1996, p. 555). Double-loop learning therefore incurs whenever the organization learns about the way it learns. Previous research indicates that double-loop learning is highly influenced by the extent of how an organization uses probes or experiments in its business processes (e.g., Argyris 1983). Double-loop learning is a central part of so-called dynamic capabilities, which an organization possesses when it has the "capacity to renew competences so as to achieve congruence with the changing business environment" (Teece, Pisano, and Shuen 1997, p. 514). In other words, dynamic capabilities are an organization's architectural skills (see also Figure 19), which enable the organization to learn that the previous capabilities have become obsolete and need to be changed. Therefore, dynamic capabilities are strategic business processes aimed at changing and redeploying other capabilities. These are interrelated with double-loop learning. Again, the capability of the organization to respond to the continuous updating of the organizational information set is of utmost importance.

3.1.5 Ranking Capabilities: Architectural and Component Capabilities

In order to understand why certain companies succeed in achieving a sustainable competitive advantage research within the RBV has historically been preoccupied with ranking capabilities (because these are the focal point of corporate uniqueness). The core belief is that not all capabilities influence competitive advantage in equal proportions. The literature in general differentiates between lower and higher level capabilities (e.g., Grant 2002) depending on their particular contribution to organizational competitive advantage. Here the terminology from Tallman and Fladmoe-Lindquist (2002) shall be utilized. They differentiate between "component capabilities" and "architectural capabilities" as illustrated in Figure 19.

Figure 19: Component and Architectural Capabilities

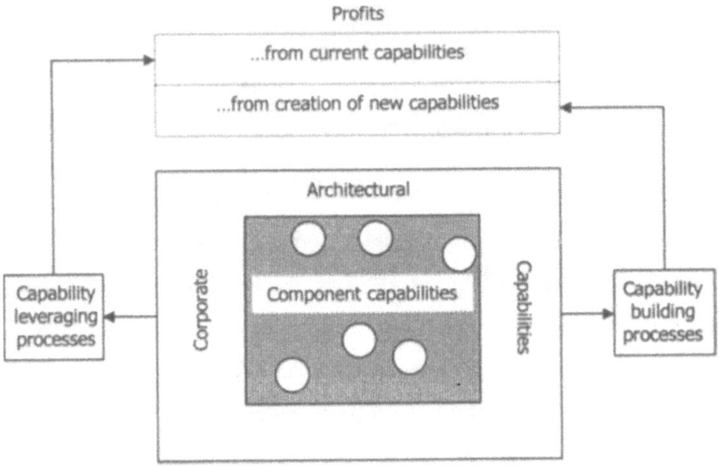

Source: adapted from Tallman and Fladmoe-Lindquist (2002, p. 119), own creation

The component capabilities are the strategic business processes in the organization. Tallman and Fladmoe-Lindquist (2002, p. 119) define the architectural capabilities as: "organization-wide routines for integrating the components of the organization to productive purposes." According to this view the most important capabilities are the architectural ones, which integrate other capabilities. The architectural capabilities perform two basic tasks: leveraging existing capabilities and developing new organizational capabilities (here is implicit the notion of dynamic capabilities). Not depicted, but equally important, are the individual organizational assets at the centre of the grey area in Figure 19.

A particular architectural capability, which is of central interest in the RBV, is the "core competence" first termed by Prahalad and Hamel (1990, p. 82), which characterize a core competence as epitomizing: "the collective learning in the organization, especially how to coordinate diverse production skills and integrate multiple streams of technologies." The quote takes up the previously mentioned importance of organizational learning and the ability to integrate business processes. In terms of Figure 19 the core competence is an architectural capability. Prahalad and Hamel (1990) further state three tests for identifying a core competence. First, it provides access to a wide variety of markets and thereby resembles as a platform (see also Kogut and Kulatilaka 1994). A core competence can therefore leverage existing capabilities and help develop new capabilities to generate rents. Second, it makes a significant contribution to perceived customer benefits. A core competence is derived from the market. I.e., it is the customer(s), who indirectly determine what the core competences are. A core competence helps the corporation fulfil the CSF(s) better than competition. Alternatively a core competence has a disproportionate influence on the efficiency, with which the value for the customer(s) is achieved. Third, it should be difficult for competitors to imitate. This is a trait, which core competences share with capabilities in general as discussed previously.

3.1.6 Modularity and Capabilities

A final point, which shall be briefly discussed here, is the use of modularity and networks. As discussed in the previous chapter the set-based development models implicitly assume some form of modularity in the underlying product. Baldwin and Clark (2002) show formally that a modularized design is always more valuable than a non-modularized design assuming no extra investment costs with setting up the platform. With positive investment costs in setting up the platform for the modularized design there is no longer a clear-cut answer. The investment costs of an automotive platform may be extremely high. Ulrich and Eppinger (2000, p. 43) estimate that the development of a platform may require between 2 and 10 times the outlay compared to point-based development. There consequently exists a trade-off between the value of increased flexibility in the product design, which must be weighed against the platform investment costs. This trade-off can be traced back to some of the first works concerning modularity (see, e.g., Starr 1965) and is similar to the trade-off previously discussed in relation with Figure 18. Solving this trade-off, though, is more difficult.

To date, a good example of modularity can be found in the computer industry's experiences with modular product architectures. Moreover the computer industry has shown the economic viability of working together in networks with partners developing and producing particular products utilizing a modular setup. Häcki and Lighton (2001) refer to so-called "network orchestrators" such as Cisco, Charles Schwab, CNET Networks, eBay, E*Trade, Palm, and Qualcomm, who all engaged in extensive cooperations with partners using a modular product architecture. In order for this cooperation to ultimately yield rents (from a theoretical viewpoint), Figure 19 provides some guidance. The long-term competitive advantage lies in the architectural capabilities as these integrate other component capabilities. The economic appeal of using networks lies therefore in the potential access to partner companies' capabilities and assets. These are then managed and integrated into the company's own business processes employing the architectural capabilities. For the cooperation to be economically sensible it is therefore crucial that the company does not loose control of its architectural capabilities as a result of the cooperation. A necessary requisite for any corporate evaluation of the economic viability of a given cooperation is consequently a consciousness about where it wishes to build "competence leadership" as Prahalad and Hamel (1990) point out. An example from the retailing industry in this respect is given by Stalk, Philip, and Shulman (1992) concerning Wal-Mart, who decided to own its transportation fleet in contrast to Kmart, who subcontracted it. Wal-Mart viewed itself as having an (architectural) capability in its logistics management system, which necessitated full ownership of the transportation assets (see Stalk, Philip, and Shulman 1992).

An example of a successful cooperation in the automobile industry is given by Adler, Goldoftas, and Levine (1999) in their empirical study of NUMMI, an auto assembly plant founded as a joint venture between Toyota and GM in California. Adler, Goldoftas, and Levine (1999, p. 57) remark on how Toyota[33] cooperated with suppliers and state that Toyota prioritized "the ability to harness suppliers' innovative capabilities and to fine-

[33] Responsible for day-to-day operations of the joint venture

tune part designs... and worked with them when problems arose." This is an example from the automobile production process of how Toyota used its cooperation to access its partners' capabilities, and the process was managed by Toyota employing its architectural capabilities.

From a theoretical viewpoint there are additional costs, which arise from using a network of independent companies. These are transaction costs (Coase 1937 and Arrow 1969) and agency costs (Jensen and Meckling 1976 and Arrow 1985), which arise from using the market. They are multiplied to the extent that the company network is utilized.

Of particular interest here are the agency costs, as they are related to the behavioural uncertainty mentioned in chapter 2. The agency costs belong to the research field economics of information (see, e.g., Stiglitz 2000 for an overview) and arise both within and outside the developing company. They can be characterized as an economic shortfall due to behavioural uncertainty resulting from information asymmetry.

Three potential types of information asymmetries are normally identified (Laffont and Martimort 2002): 1) hidden characteristics, 2) hidden action and hidden information, and 3) hidden intention. Consequently three potential agency problems can arise, which cause agency costs: 1) adverse selection, 2) moral hazard, and 3) hold up. There are also three categories of solutions to the potential agency problems:

1) solution to hidden characteristics: signalling, screening, and self selection
2) solution to hidden action and hidden information: profit participation and monitoring
3) solution to hidden intention: finding appropriate incentive structures

In the case of cooperating with suppliers the first type arise when the developing company is in the process of searching for potential suppliers for the development project, whereas the final two types arise during the course of a cooperation with a supplier.

Viewing the supplier cooperation from the viewpoint of information economics makes it evident that the developing company no longer has full control of the component capabilities, which have been integrated and lie outside the firm's boundary (see also Figure 19). The above discussion of not loosing control of the architectural capabilities is therefore here also of relevance. The additional cost factors must be traded off against the added value of accessing the partner companies' capabilities. The particular issues resulting from the information economics approach shall be discussed at the end of chapter 3.

3.2 Empirical Research of Automotive Development Processes

From the above outline of capabilities and core competencies it is clear that the automobile development process (as depicted in the previous chapter) fits many of the mentioned characteristics needed for attaining a sustainable competitive advantage. This is because the automobile development process presents a highly complex undertaking with many managerial alternatives for shaping organizational learning and leveraging and developing organizational capabilities. Indeed Prahalad and Hamel (1990) argue for the unique role of the product development process in helping a corporation meet its CSFs better than the competition in terms of core competence. The purpose of the following sections is therefore to analyze how the automobile development process can be used to achieve a sustainable competitive advantage from the viewpoint of the above outlined strategic management models, the main emphasis being on the RBV. Of particular interest are select empirical studies conducted in the automobile industry. These shall serve as a data basis for the analysis.

3.2.1 Using Prototypes to Achieve Internal and External Integration

Based on their extensive research in the global automobile industry, Clark and Fujimoto (1991) and Wheelwright and Clark (1992) identify three main forces shaping the competitive environment. First of all, international competition has increased due to a combination of emerging global product segments and automotive companies both willing and capable of competing internationally. A prime example of the increased competition is the US market where very dominant US firms in the past are now increasingly loosing market share to Japanese and European automotive companies. Second of all, customers are growing more demanding, and yesterday's CSFs have become today's minimum requirements in terms of customer buying criteria. In other words, the bar is continually being raised for market participation. Apart from expecting good performance from a car, customers are increasingly also expecting a product, which satisfies them at a deeper level in terms of designs nuances, sounds, etc.. Third of all, technology has improved steadily. However, the effect of technology is more subtle. Partly as a result of networked relationships in the automobile industry growing more powerful, it is no longer possible to build a sustainable competitive advantage around technological assets alone. Rather, the way technology is put to use during the development process is of importance. I.e., the corporate capabilities and the leverage of these are decisive. Companies must therefore integrate technology within the automobile in a sensible way and at the same time integrate customers' requirements into the automotive design. These are the before mentioned aspects of internal and external integrity respectively. All factors have contributed to a steady rise in the uncertainty, which both effects the external and internal environment surrounding the automobile development process. Moreover, as world-class manufacturing strategies are no longer exceptional, increasingly companies in the automobile industry must gain a competitive advantage through extraordinary mastery of the development process. In other words, the development process has become the focal point of industrial competition (Clark and Fujimoto 1991).

Due to the difficult and labour-intensive process of accessing firm-specific information about the development process, there is little extensive and recent research available on the automobile development process. The main sources in the following shall be Clark and Fujimoto's (1991) and Ellison et al.'s (1995) comparative studies of 29 automotive development projects in 20 major companies worldwide (US, Europe, Japan) as well as Sobek's (1997) comparative study of the automotive development processes at Chrysler and Toyota. These studies have been chosen because they yield in-depth insights into the objectives and business processes comprising the automobile development process at the various companies. The data is therefore sufficiently abundant for it to be used as an input for the subsequent models. By incorporating the findings from the research the preceding sections concerning competitive advantage can be weighed against empirical observations of the automotive development process. As previously mentioned the objective is ultimately to model the automobile development process using a quantitative valuation model building upon the theory from financial economics.

The following sections shall explore the circumstances under which the three previously outlined development models (point-based development, point-based concurrent development and set-based concurrent development) are put to use in practice. Historically, Toyota started employing concurrent development in the 1960s, Mazda and Nissan followed in the 1970s and 1980s respectively (Ward et al. 1995), and most US and European firms were utilizing concurrent development models by the middle of the 1990s (Ellison et al. 1995). The main emphasis in the following will therefore be on the point-based concurrent engineering model and the set-based concurrent engineering model presented earlier.

The methodology employed by Clark and Fujimoto (1991) is to compare the surveyed companies on the three overall objectives (time, productivity and integrity) for the development process utilizing statistical measures. Their research covered the time frame from 1985 to the end of the 1980s. Clark and Fujimoto (1991, p. 77) find that Japanese companies on average lead in terms of development productivity followed by a mix of European and US firms. In terms of development lead time (Clark and Fujimoto 1991, p. 78) European and US companies must on average start the development process 5 years ahead of the market introduction whereas Japanese companies on average can wait until 3.5 years before market introduction with starting the development process. In both productivity and lead time the Japanese companies therefore are in the lead. European and US companies share the second place with no clear regional leadership. Regarding the final performance variable, product integrity, there is no clear regional leadership (Clark and Fujimoto 1991, p. 85). On an intra-regional level the highest product integrity is achieved by selected European and Japanese companies. The second place is likewise shared, with the remaining European, US, and Japanese companies being mixed in the ranking. Apparently it is possible to develop high quality (integrity) and technically superior automobiles while not necessarily being at the top of either the lead time or productivity rankings.

The frame for this work shall be a comparison of development performance in terms of the outlined development models (in particular the point- and set-based concurrent models of development). In order to do this, the development funnel (see Figure 14) can be thought of as a simplifying instrument. As discussed earlier, the various employed development processes in practice can be thought of as representing different shapes of respective development funnels. The development funnel can be characterized according to the number of design alternatives being developed in parallel and the way management narrows the funnel during the development phases. The number of prototypes developed during the development process can be employed as an indicator for the number of design alternatives being developed. In general, none of the surveyed automotive companies apply either the point- or set-based models solely for their development process. Rather, each company can be portrayed as utilizing each of the models to a greater or lesser extent depending on the specific project at hand.

As mentioned earlier prototypes play an important role in exploring the design space. Of particular interest is therefore whether it is possible to infer an advantage in development process performance through the use of prototypes. Empirically, Clark and Fujimoto (1991) find clear differences in the total number of prototypes being developed by the companies in their study (see Table 5).

Table 5: Number of Prototypes

Region / *Number of*	*Japan*	*US*	*Europe*	
			Volume producer	*High-End specialist*
Engineering prototypes	38	34	37	54
Pilot vehicle prototypes	53	129	109	205

Source: Own creation, adapted from Clark and Fujimoto (1991, p. 196)

In Table 5 the row "Engineering prototypes" refers to the number of prototypes employed during the development process up until the point in time where the final automotive design has been developed (i.e., the "product design" phase in Figure 5). The row "Pilot vehicle prototypes" refers to the number of prototypes being built of the final automotive design. There are two aspects of these results. First, the number of prototypes employed before the final automotive design is on average roughly the same, with the European premium brands being the exception. Second, compared to Japanese companies, US and European (high-end) companies build two times and four times as many pilot vehicle prototypes respectively. Clark and Fujimoto (1991, p. 196) note that: "This suggests that each Japanese prototype is a more powerful problem-solving tool." In other words, it is the way the prototypes are utilized as problem-solving tools that help explain the Japanese advantages in productivity and lead time. As discussed above, the outcome of the problem-solving cycles is a gradual narrowing of the development funnel as the less superior design alternatives (prototypes) are sorted out.

Clark and Fujimoto (1991) identify the primary source of competitive advantage in the use of an "integrated" development process as an aid in narrowing the funnel. They explored the use of internal integration, external integration, and cross-functional business processes in the surveyed companies (see Table 6).

Table 6: Integrated Development and Specialization

Region / *Index*	*Japan*	*US*	*Europe*	
			Volume producer	*High-End specialist*
Internal integration	7.6	4.6	2.8	3.2
External integration	4.4	0.8	2.0	2.5
Involvement of long-term participants	523	1190	863	817

Source: adapted from Clark and Fujimoto (1991, p. 267)

On average the Japanese companies scored significantly higher on both internal and external integration. I.e., they succeeded in developing an automotive design with good internal technical consistency between the parts and modules and at the same time integrating the customers' buying criteria more fully than the US and European companies. The final row of Table 6 shows the Japanese companies using a lower number of long-term project participants than either US or European companies. Clark and Fujimoto (1991) therefore propose the use of cross-functional business processes in terms of less reliance on specialists as being a key driver for achieving such a high degree of integration. In order to achieve effective problem-solving processes, these must include and optimally respond to all relevant external and internal sources of information, not only the information existing in a given development function. In other words, the cross-functional approach enables the organization to better assess its combined information asset.

Clark and Fujimoto (1991) also find high levels of positive correlation between the degree of integration and both the lead-time and productivity indicators. A universal theme and key result of Clark and Fujimoto's (1991) work is therefore that the overall pattern of consistency of the automobile development process leads to a competitive advantage. Only through a simultaneous focus by management on "both the whole and the parts" (Clark and Fujimoto 1991, p. 352) can a company develop automobiles in a timely and productive manner. A similar result is given by the studies on development performance presented in Wheelwright and Clark (1992, p. 26). They state that: "The challenge of integration applies ...at the working level within... work groups with different disciplines, tasks, and experiences." The final focus of management must therefore be on the implementation of an integrated problem-solving process at the working level. Still, Wheelwright and Clark (1992, p. 175) note that an integrated development process is particularly important in business environments where "markets and technologies are more dynamic and time is a more critical element of competition." This is not the case when the corporation is in an environment where "product designs are stable (or change only in a minor way), customer requirements are well defined, the interfaces between functions are clear and well established, and lifecycles and lead times are long." (Wheelwright and Clark 1992, p. 175). In such an environment "functional groups may develop new products effectively with a modest amount of coordination through procedures and the occasional meeting." (Wheelwright and Clark (1992, p. 175). It seems therefore that the uncertainty of project value drivers determines the need for a more integrated development process. Reviewing the results of Clark and Fujimoto (1991) from this perspective, one could conclude that the highly positive effect of integrated development observed in the automobile development processes was partly an outcome of uncertain internal and external environments at the time of the empirical research.

Having observed above the importance of an integrated development process and the very different uses of prototypes during the development process, it is still essential to explore how management narrows the development funnel while at the same time focusing on high degrees of internal and external integrity. This is a principal question, which the product development literature seeks to solve. Wheelwright and Clark (1992, p. 16) propose that it is management which "fosters internal integration and integrates customer needs into the details of design. Effective product development is not the result of a single individual, but strong leadership makes a difference." The role of leadership in the automobile development process is therefore to connect and employ the sources of internal and external knowledge in the problem-solving process in order to achieve a timely and productive development process. The issue, which would need to be examined, is therefore the extent to which management can shape automotive product development performance by utilizing either a point- or set-based concurrent development strategy.

3.2.2 Observed Point- and Set-Based Development Processes

As was observed above it is the way prototypes are applied within the development process, which most likely influences product development performance. The following sections will primarily deal with the empirical findings regarding the point- and set-based development strategies in this respect. At the beginning of the development process in the "concept development" and "system-level design" phases (see Figure 4) many Japanese and US companies employ a set-based approach (Ward et al. 1995). These companies therefore purposefully use different designs (prototypes) of the complete vehicle in order to explore the design-space. This is equivalent to widening up the development funnel (see Figure 14) in the first development phases. On average they construct three different 1/5 scale clay models of the complete vehicle. This is also the case at Chrysler (Sobek 1997). Toyota is an exception in the worldwide automobile industry. They build many more 1/5 models. Sobek (1997) reports that Toyota builds between five and twenty different models in the concept phase. Toyota's development funnel is therefore apparently characterized by a relatively wide mouth and resulting extensive exploration of the design space. Toyota is therefore "front-loading" its development process whereas the industry norm seems to be building an increasing number of prototypes as time passes. This would explain the high number of prototypes built (see Table 5).

A second aspect of the development funnel is the way management narrows it passing through the design stages. Sobek (1997, p. 118) reports that e.g., Chrysler at the end of the concept phase has made "all the major decisions regarding the vehicle architecture [including] door configuration, power train configurations, overall appearance, hard points, suspension points and travel, and locations for all the parts within the vehicle." Likewise Chrysler had at the end of the concept phase decided on most on the major suppliers. This means that Chrysler narrows the development funnel very quickly compared to Toyota where Sobek (1997) observed a much slower narrowing of the funnel. On a subsystem (e.g., suspension springs, exhaust systems, power train, etc.) level Toyota routinely has 10 different design alternatives open for review as late as the first vehicle prototype (i.e., during the "Testing and refinement" phase, see also Figure 4). If there is a high degree of uncertainty in the development project (e.g., a new automobile platform) Toyota uses an above-average number of designs/prototypes (Sobek 1997). At the end of the testing and refinement phase Toyota decides on the final vehicle design including all subsystem designs. Thus the Toyota design philosophy implies postponing design decisions until "the last possible moment without delaying the project." (Sobek 1997, p. 97). In effect Toyota therefore practices a slow narrowing of the development funnel with many more (compared to the industry average) design alternatives being developed in parallel. The characterized development funnels are illustrated figuratively in Figure 20.

Figure 20: Observed Automobile Development Funnels

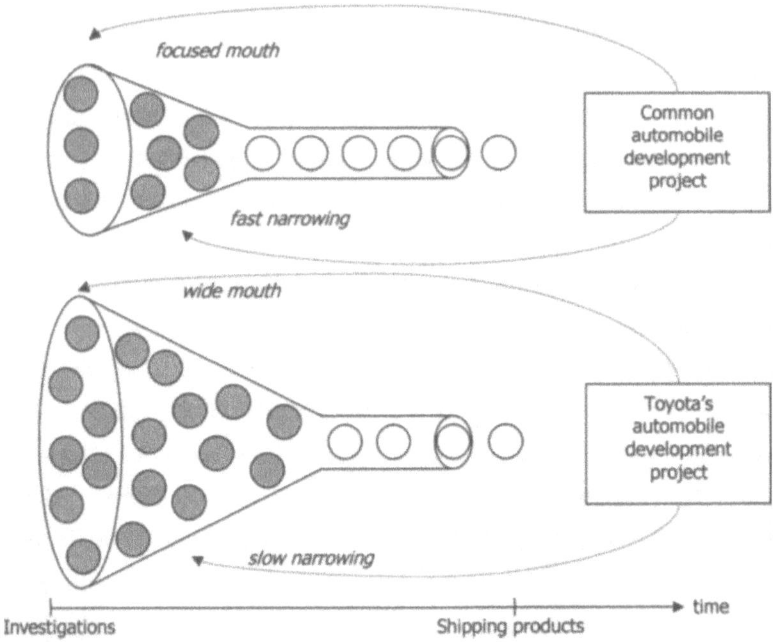

Source: own creation

Though, for the development of some subsystems Toyota follows an approach similar to the upper development funnel in Figure 20. This type of development process at Toyota is the so-called "rapid inch-up" strategy, which Clark and Wheelwright (1992, p. 38) describe as: "frequent, small changes in technology that cumulatively lead to continuous performance improvement." Ward et al. (1995, p. 51) further found that Toyota keeps "many of the subsystems and components essentially the same, while selectively innovating." A set-based process with a lower number of design alternatives developed concurrently therefore makes it possible for Toyota to focus its resources and investments in areas where it sees the highest potential. Rapid inch-up is essentially a point-based concurrent development strategy with primarily one main design alternative being developed through an emphasis on fast problem-solving cycles. The number of designs developed in parallel is accordingly relatively low and the funnel is narrowed more quickly. Ward et al. (1995) describe how Toyota applied the rapid inch-up strategy in the development of a gearshift lever. In this case the design space was purposefully explored only to a small degree. E.g., the mounting holes for the lever had not changed for years. Only marginal improvements were pursued and implemented. Ward et al. (1995, p. 56) state that the rapid inch-up strategy is applied when the design-problem at hand is characterized by "technological stability, limited interface with other components, and relatively simple geometry." This is the case with a gearshift lever.

In general, some potential problems remain if a company chooses to develop using a point-based model (Wheelwright and Clark 1992 and Ward et al. 1995):

1) First of all, there is the above-mentioned problem of not having explored the design space more fully. Ward et al. (1995, p. 59) therefore state: "Rapid inch-up can find only 'local optima' – the best possible design based on the current fundamental concept." Inevitably point-based engineering will pass through problem-solving cycles without a systematic and broad exploration of the potential advantages of fundamentally different design alternatives.

2) Second of all, there is the problem of low integrity, which depends on the degree of concurrency between the activities in the various development stages (see also Figure 11). If there is no clear project leadership in order to both employ and develop cross-functional business processes then the point-based process will not adequately bring the internal and external information available into the decision-making process. In practice this often implies a suboptimal utilization of prototypes. I.e., the developing organization fails to incorporate information from early prototyping cycles for downstream decisions. Wheelwright and Clark (1992, p. 272) observed: "While some information gets transferred from one cycle to another in the physical prototype units, it is much less than is available and much less than might be transferred."

3) Third of all, probably the most important system-wide effect of point-based development is the pattern of decision-making in which management makes wide-

ranging irreversible decisions regarding vehicle architecture before uncertainty is resolved, e.g., in the exemplified development process at Chrysler. In the case of negative information as an outcome of the design-build-cycle, management often has no other choice than to invest in costly late-minute changes to the design. This is often the case in practice. Due to the path-dependent nature of the automobile development process, it is very difficult to roll back initial decisions without incurring substantial extra development costs. Most automobile companies following a point-based process are aware of this and therefore build a large number of prototypes at the end of the development process in order to realize higher degrees of internal and external integrity (see also Table 5). Therefore the costs of automobile development are greatly increased due to the combination of prototypes in general becoming more expensive as time passes (see Figure 8), and the number of prototypes increasing simultaneously. Interestingly, Clark and Fujimoto (1991) discovered that US and European companies following a more point-based approach were also the ones building a large number of prototypes late in the development process. Nonetheless, this did not help them avoid comparatively low degrees of integrity (as seen in Table 6).

3.2.3 Toyota's Three Principles for Set-Based Development

The following sections shall deal in detail with the set-based concurrent model of development in practice. As was mentioned above the set-based model is implemented to varying degrees in the automobile industry. In dealing with the set-based development model in more detail, particularly the development practices at Toyota shall be outlined and discussed. Sobek's (1997) research at Toyota in Japan describes a development process, which is markedly set-based in its approach to exploring the design space and managing the development funnel. This research was the basis for several follow-up articles (e.g., Sobek, Ward, and Liker 1999), each outlining some extraordinary development practices. Toyota is highly respected by many executives in the automobile industry for their prowess in developing and producing automobiles of high integrity, quickly, and efficiently (see, e.g., Appendix 1 and Clark and Fujimoto 1991). At the same time the Toyota development system has in the literature been called a "paradox" (Sobek, Ward, and Liker 1999). The reason for this is best illustrated using Figure 18. By utilizing a set-based approach the investment costs are higher than is the case utilizing a point-based approach and if the value of flexibility is not taken into account, the resulting development system would seem very inefficient, i.e., it would have a large negative NPV.

Sobek, Ward, and Liker (1999) have identified three design principles (shown in Figure 21), which together form the framework, which Toyota applies in order to manage the development funnel.

Figure 21: Toyota's Three Design Principles

1. *Map the design space*
    - Define feasible regions
    - Explore trade-offs by designing multiple alternatives
    - Communicate sets of possibilities
2. *Integrate by intersection*
    - Look for intersections of feasible sets
    - Impose minimum constraint
    - Seek conceptual robustness
3. *Establish feasibility before commitment*
    - Narrow sets gradually while increasing detail
    - Stay within sets once committed
    - Control by managing uncertainty at process gates

Source: Sobek, Ward, and Liker (1999, p. 73)

3.2.3.1 Toyota's 1st Design Principle: Mapping the Design Space

In order to develop an automobile Toyota first maps the design space. They do so using so-called engineering checklists, which form explicit ranges of design alternatives. In other words, the first principle is focused on widening the mouth of the development funnel. A checklist for a particular automotive part e.g., specifies recommended thickness of the material, minimum strength characteristics, reliability, and so on. A checklist can also contain relevant information about work processes such as for instance ways to add value in terms of solutions to past problems, suggestions to improve costs and quality, etc.. The checklists at Toyota embody much information about the design space, which in other companies is largely tacit (refer to Sobek's 1997 research at Chrysler and to Nonaka 1990 regarding tacit and explicit organizational information). As uncertainty (technical and market) resolves with time the checklists are updated to reflect the current state of the explored design space. Ward et al. (1995, pp. 56-57) notice: "Toyota is updating and refining its map of the design space before making decisions." Toyota's checklists therefore can be viewed as representing physical embodiments of the organizational learning process.

At the outset of the automotive development process the checklists for the various automotive subsystems are used to create discrete design alternatives, which in effect represent the mouth of the development funnel. The communication of these design alternatives to other process participants often takes place in the shape of selection matrices (termed by Pugh 1991), which can be viewed as explicit combinations of individual checklists in order to compare individual design alternatives with the relative performance of their evaluation criteria (see Figure 22). The underlying idea is paralled very much by the work done by Akao in the 1960's, based on research done at, amongst others, Toyota in Japan. A key challenge is to incorporate the purchase criteria of the customer into the product design. As a result, forms of selection matrices are often deployed within the Quality Function Deployment (QFD) paradigm (see, e.g., Akao 1990).

Figure 22: Toyota's Selection Matrix

	Function 1	*Function* 2	*Durability*	*Space*	E(PV)	σ
A	○	○	△	✕	100	10 %
B	△	△	**○**	○	90	30 %
C	○	△	△	**○**	110	5 %

○ - Excellent ○ - Acceptable △ - Marginal ✕ - Unacceptable

Note: the correlation matrix between the Present Values of the three alternatives has not been depicted and would have to be taken into consideration as part of an overall valuation model for the automotive development process.

Source: adapted from Sobek, Ward, and Liker (1999, p. 76) and own creation

Thus the selection matrix in Figure 22 is an example of three discrete design alternatives *A*, *B*, and *C*. Each is compared from the viewpoint of two involved functions (1 and 2) and according to two key technical performance variables (durability and space). Finally, the matrix contains the two last columns, which were added by this author. These final variables are the expected present values and the standard deviation of expected present values respectively. Their purpose is to link the evaluation criteria of the automotive design to the financial markets and thereby to company owners. This approach explicitly incorporates the financial markets view of the development process as an important input to ensure an optimal valuation and controlling of the process. Utilized as a general framework for communicating design alternatives, Figure 22 can be adapted to whatever projects the automotive company is considering. Each row in Figure 22 corresponds to a discrete design alternative and has the information needed to represent the design alternatives and therefore also the basis for making informed decisions about resource allocation. In the case of Figure 22 management would choose to further develop either one or both of the design alternatives *B* and *C* as the alternative *A* is eliminated due to unacceptable performance in the "space" dimension. In the example in Figure 22 more than one alternative is viable. In this case the literature does not give a sole answer concerning a general model of choice to influence resource allocation. An important part of this work is concerned with developing a quantitative model for solving this resource allocation problem, partly based on the information contained in a setup similar to Figure 22.

3.2.3.2 Toyota's 2nd Design Principle: Integrate by Intersection

Toyota's second design principle regards the choice between the various design alternatives in the selection matrix. That is, the second principle is concerned with achieving high degrees of internal and external integrity. Toyota seeks to find feasible areas of the design space by focusing on the intersections between design evaluation criteria. In other words, Toyota concentrates on finding optimal system-wide design alternatives.

An important part of the second principle is concerned with managing uncertainty. As time passes and information about technical and market uncertainties is revealed, the relative advantages of each design alternative shifts. In Figure 22 the extent to which uncertainty affects the optimality of a design alternative is given by the size of σ, which is determined by the evolution of information. The uncertainties are in this case the combined effects of market and technical uncertainty (see Figure 18). In the example design alternative *B* shows the highest degree of uncertainty (σ_B = 30%) followed by design alternatives *A* (σ_A = 10%) and *C* (σ_C = 5%). As pointed out earlier it is the way management utilizes prototypes, which yields information about the viability of a given design alternative. Toyota seems to have two main ways of dealing with the uncertainty inherent in the development process. Both are concerned with the utilization of prototypes. First, Toyota is "deliberately delaying specifications... to make last-minute adjustments" (Sobek, Ward, and Liker 1999, p. 77). Consequently, at any given point in time Toyota imposes minimum constraint. The design alternatives are not constrained more than is necessary for the design alternatives to be feasible. A general manager of body engineering at Toyota once stated: "The manager's job is to prevent people from making decisions too quickly." (Ward et al. 1995, p. 48). This first aspect is consequently concerned with the timing of the investment decisions. That is, the managerial flexibility in the resource allocation process is deemed important in the light of an uncertain automotive development process. Second, as mentioned above Toyota utilizes sets of design alternatives in parallel to a much greater extent than other automotive firms. This allows Toyota to choose between several alternatives instead of being reliant on a single design alternative. A general manger of styling at Toyota pointed out that they "prefer lots of torpedoes to a single sniper bullet." (Ward et al. 1995, p. 47). This second aspect is consequently concerned with the added value of being able to choose the most valuable design alternative once the designs have been developed. This parallels strongly the 'Value of flexibility to switch)' part in Figure 18.

The final aspect of the second design principle is preoccupied with how to compose the original set of design alternatives. Toyota composes the set of design alternatives in such a way that it is "conceptually robust" (Sobek, Ward, and Liker 1999, p. 79). For the set-based strategy to work it is essential for the development process to stay within the set. An essential component of staying within the sets is Toyota's use of its checklists (Ward et al. 1995). If however the selected set of alternatives contains no feasible option then the developing company would risk an absolute failure.[34] This challenge parallels a known problem from portfolio theory. It can be shown that the not only the individual sources of uncertainty (the σ of a design alternative) is important for total portfolio risk but also the correlation matrix plays a role (see Markowitz 1952). It remains to be seen if this result can be replicated in a valuation model of the automobile development process.

[34] Essentially in this case the company would either have to start the development process over again as none of the alternatives could be implemented or proceed with the best design alternative in a point-based fashion. Both situations would most likely mean large delays in development time and large amounts of extra investments in order to finish the automobile.

3.2.3.3 Toyota's 3rd Design Principle: Establish Feasibility before Commitment

Toyota's third and final design principle is concerned with the important task of narrowing the development funnel. Knowing when to abandon a design alternative and focus on the remaining alternative(s) becomes crucial. That is, the third design principle is also about timing resource allocation decisions.

At Toyota Sobek, Ward, and Liker (1999, p. 79) observed: "Knowing when to decide becomes a central task of the project manager (the chief engineer at Toyota)." Narrowing the funnel is a key responsibility of the chief engineer at Toyota. Sobek (1997, p. 84) states: "in every interview, engineers referred to the CE [chief engineer], not his staff, as the decision-maker." Sobek (1997) also found that the chief engineer at Toyota possesses at least the three following qualities: above average technical understanding of technical issues, good leadership qualities, and a strong understanding of the company. Toyota manages the development process through a series of gates. At each gate the chief engineer decides what design alternatives are the most promising and has the authority to abandon suboptimal alternatives. The chief engineer is therefore literally the gatekeeper and is said to be using his extensive knowledge of the company and the market place in making his decisions.

Toyota's previously mentioned use of prototypes plays a central role at the development gates. At Toyota, Ward et al. (1995, p. 50) observed: "At each milestone [gate], a physical product integrates the work of all the parts of the company." For some subsystems Toyota has less emphasis on working with sets and relatively quickly decides on a design alternative. This is the case for transmissions, which are relatively expensive. For other subsystems Toyota works with sets and narrows the funnel slowly. This is the case for exhaust systems, which are relatively inexpensive. Accordingly, Toyota purposefully switches between development models depending on the problem at hand.

3.2.4 Involving Suppliers in the Automotive Development Process

The final feature of automotive development in practice, which shall be dealt with in the following, is the involvement of suppliers in the development process. Suppliers play an increasingly important role in the automotive development process. Clark and Fujimoto (1991) found large discrepancies in the way automotive companies involved suppliers in the development process (see Figure 23). The extent to which a potential competitive advantage can be accomplished through the use of suppliers is therefore the focus of the following sections.

Figure 23: Involving Suppliers in the Engineering Effort

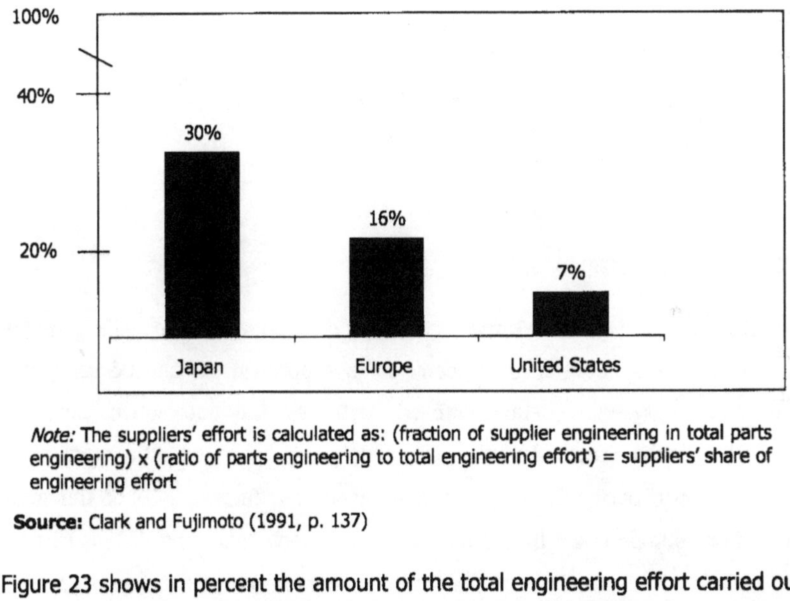

Note: The suppliers' effort is calculated as: (fraction of supplier engineering in total parts engineering) x (ratio of parts engineering to total engineering effort) = suppliers' share of engineering effort

Source: Clark and Fujimoto (1991, p. 137)

Figure 23 shows in percent the amount of the total engineering effort carried out by the automotive company's suppliers. There are apparent differences across the regions. By far, the Japanese automotive companies studied involve their suppliers most extensively and on average have them undertaking 30% of the total product development engineering. Clark and Fujimoto (1991) also studied the types of parts produced by suppliers (see Figure 24).

Figure 24: Types of Parts Produced by Suppliers

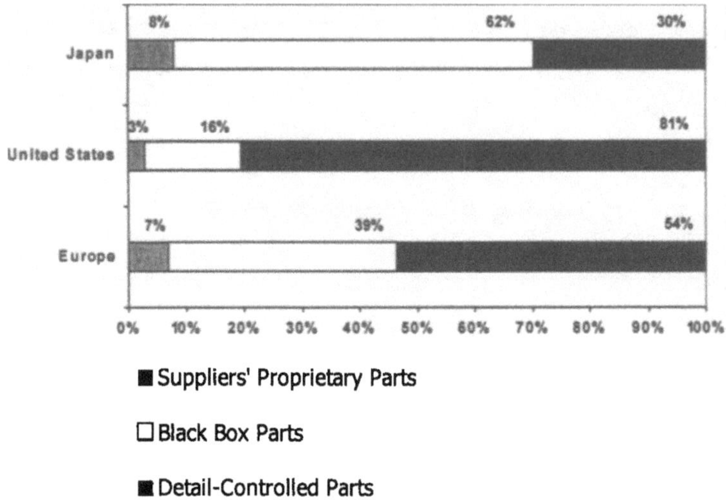

Source: Clark and Fujimoto (1991, p. 145)

The aspect of interest in Figure 24 is the engineering development effort, which can be performed either by the automotive company or its supplier(s). As can be seen, the parts completely engineered (detail-controlled parts) by the automotive company dominate in the United States. In this case, suppliers function as little more than marginal production capacity. In Europe the situation is different. 54% of the total engineering effort is undertaken by the automotive company itself, and 46% is carried out by the supplier. In Japan 70% of the total development effort is taken on by the suppliers. That is, a significant proportion of the automotive development effort lies outside the automotive company. Furthermore, Clark and Fujimoto (1991) compared the amount of total engineering undertaken by the supplier and the degree to which the automotive company explored the design space (see Figure 25).

Figure 25: Project Scope by Projects and Region

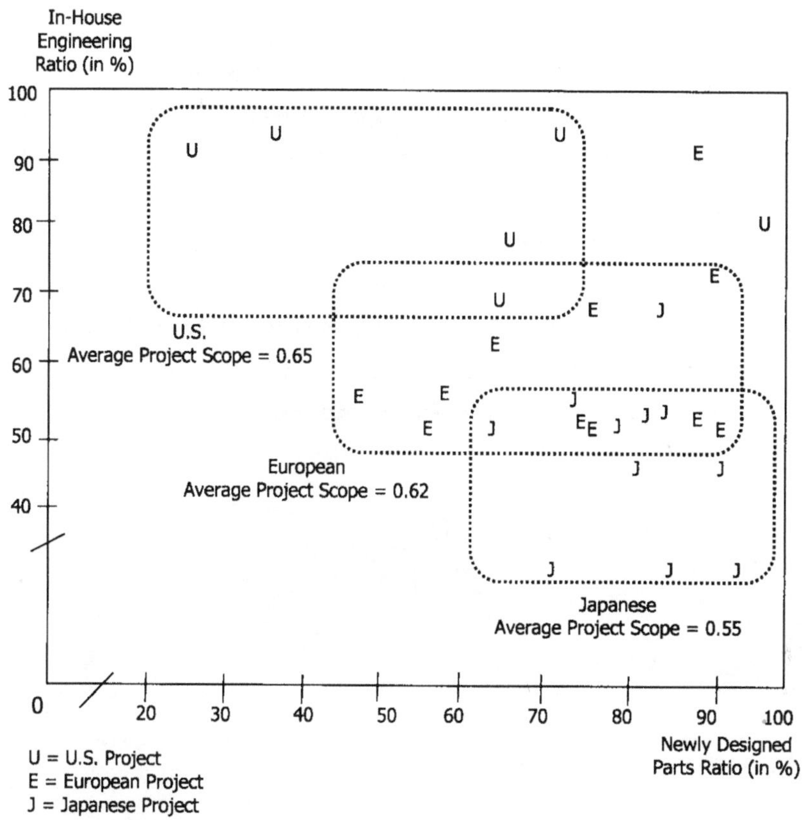

"In-House Engineering Ratio" defined as: The fraction of total engineering effort in the product accounted for by new engineering work done in-house.

Source: Clark and Fujimoto (1991, p. 151)

Figure 25 shows a positive correlation (using regression analysis) between the amount of engineering done by the supplier (1 – 'In-House Engineering Ratio') and the exploration of the design space ('newly designed parts ratio'). It can also be seen that there are roughly three strategies concerning supplier involvement, analogous to Figure 24. Clark and Fujimoto (1991) discovered that the companies utilizing suppliers engineering capabilities the most were also the ones introducing the most new parts. I.e., the Japanese companies simultaneously utilize suppliers and explore the design space the most, with European and US companies following. Wasti and Liker (1999, p. 444) state that Japanese automotive companies: "are regarded as the benchmarks for world-class practices in involving suppliers in the early stages of design." In terms of Figure 18 the negative effect ('Investment costs') of exploring additional design alternatives is partly annulled in the case of competent suppliers as they have a level of expertise in specific parts, which the automobile developing company cannot as easily match. This competence most likely translates into lower overall investment costs. At the same time the positive effect of 'Value of flexibility to switch' (in Figure 18) is taken advantage of. A last difference between Japanese (see Figure 26) and other automotive companies lies in the tiered structure of the Japanese networks.

Figure 26: Japanese Supplier Networks

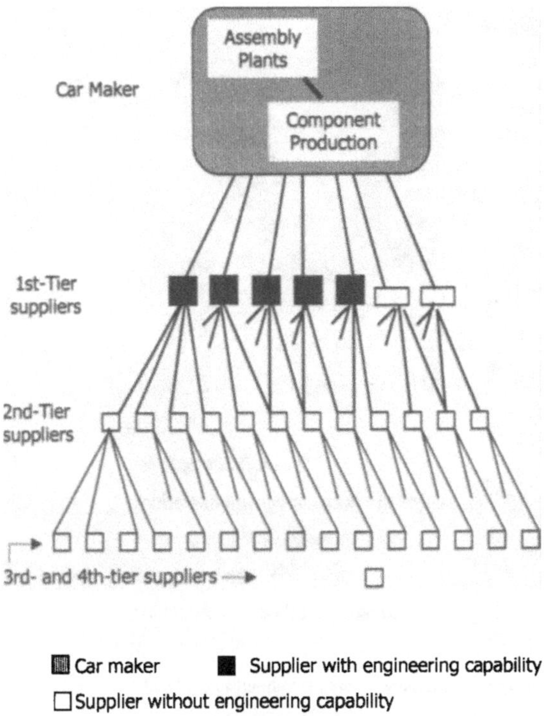

...characterized by:

-smaller in-house component operations

-lower degree of vertical integration

-long term contracts

-close communication and coordination

-smaller number of large suppliers, mostly with engineering capability

-tall hierarchy with 2nd-, 3rd-, and 4th-tier suppliers

Source: Clark and Fujimoto (1991, p. 139)

As can be seen in Figure 26 Clark and Fujimoto (1991) observed that the Japanese automotive companies used a tall hierarchy whereas US automotive companies (Figure 27) used a flat hierarchy in the supplier network.[35] The tall hierarchy in Japanese relationships coheres well with the above mentioned competent suppliers with product

[35] The last decade, though, has seen a strong decline in the number of suppliers used by North American and European automobile producers. In the 1990s they used between 700 and 900 different suppliers, whereas the number was 450 on average by 2001. (see Knowledge@Wharton 2006)

engineering competences, necessary for a valuable and lower cost exploration of the design space.

Figure 27: US Supplier Networks

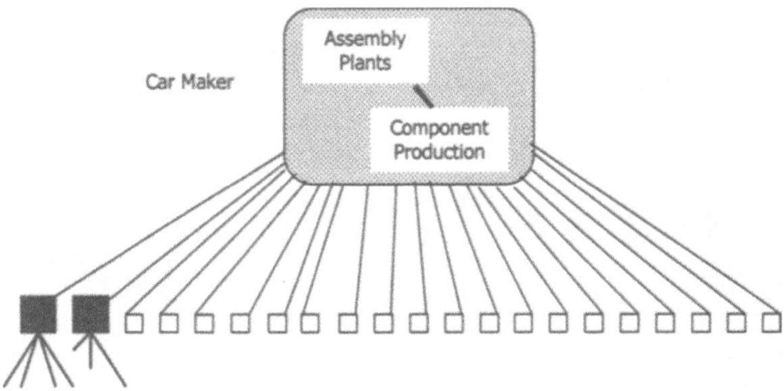

...characterized by:

-larger in-house component operations

-higher degree of vertical integration

-short term contracts

- less communication and coordination

-flat hierarchy

-larger number of small suppliers, mostly without engineering capability

-large suppliers with technical capability (minority)

■ Car maker ■ Supplier with engineering capability

□ Supplier without engineering capability

Source: Clark and Fujimoto (1991, p. 139)

This structure of US relationships most likely makes it simpler to manage the interface with suppliers in Japan than in the US. However, the Japanese companies are more dependent on a few very large suppliers while the US companies are less vulnerable to problems at a single supplier. It would therefore be likely that Japanese automotive companies in practice give a great deal of consideration to the assets and capabilities of their first tier suppliers. Indeed Wasti and Liker (1999) observed that Japanese companies look for first tier suppliers, who are capable of "building capability" (Wasti and Liker 1999, p. 445) in a longer-term relationship. Japanese first tier suppliers therefore must have a minimum of assets and capabilities in order for them to be considered. This is congruent with Clark and Fujimoto's (1991) results shown in Figure 23 and Figure 24. Due to the high degree of suppliers' engineering effort involved in the final automotive design, the suppliers must have a substantial resource base. As mentioned above, the suppliers who have a competitive advantage in certain subsystems may even be able to develop these parts better than the automotive company itself (Wasti and Liker 1999). In contrast, US supplier relationships are often characterized as 'adversarial', short term, and taking place in perfect competition. It is difficult for suppliers to differentiate themselves as most of the designs are detail-controlled parts (see Figure 24), and the relationship quickly is reduced to a competition on price. As a result of the flat hierarchy (see Figure 27) it would also be hard for the automotive company to develop more extensive relationships with each individual supplier.

3.3 Toyota's Development System – A Resource-Based Analysis

The following sections shall analyse in more detail the automotive development process at Toyota from the lens of strategic management. Very little research has been done at the Japanese headquarters of Toyota concentrating on its automotive development process. Research until now has concentrated mainly on Toyota's production system.[36] The primary source for the development system at Toyota in this context shall be Sobek (1997). In great detail he outlines the development process at Toyota and thereby provides the needed material for further analysis in this work.

[36] A recent overview is given by Spear (2004).

3.3.1 Toyota's Supplier Relationships

In general, Toyota's use of suppliers can also be characterized by the above Japanese supplier relationship. However, Toyota actually utilizes its first tier supplier base more extensively than most other automotive companies (refer in general to Liker et al. 1996, Sobek 1997, and Wasti and Liker 1999). Toyota on average buys 70% of its total vehicle value (on a cost basis) directly from suppliers (Sobek 1997). A key criterion for Toyota in choosing a supplier is the supplier's capability to work with sets in order to explore the design space more fully. A Toyota engineering general manager observed: "only some suppliers can handle the ambiguity" (Wasti and Liker 1999, p. 177) of working with multiple design alternatives for a subsystem concurrently. In fact, examples of relatively high numbers of design alternatives are reported in connection with Toyota's suppliers. Toyota therefore "does not treat all its first tier suppliers equally." (Sobek 1997, p. 102). Suppliers such as Nippondenso, which possesses a strong resource base, are highly regarded. Furthermore, as Toyota's supplier relationship "deepens with experience, it seems that the use of set-based communication and development techniques correspondingly increase." (Liker et al. 1996, p. 170). The use of set-based development practices in cooperation with the supplier is strongly correlated with a modular design setup. That is, Toyota must excel at systems engineering in order to establish an optimal platform for the cooperation.

Based on their studies, Millman and Wilson (1994) propose a positive correlation between the extent to which the cooperation is adversarial or collaborative and the level of involvement with customers (see Figure 28).

Figure 28: Supplier Relational Development Model

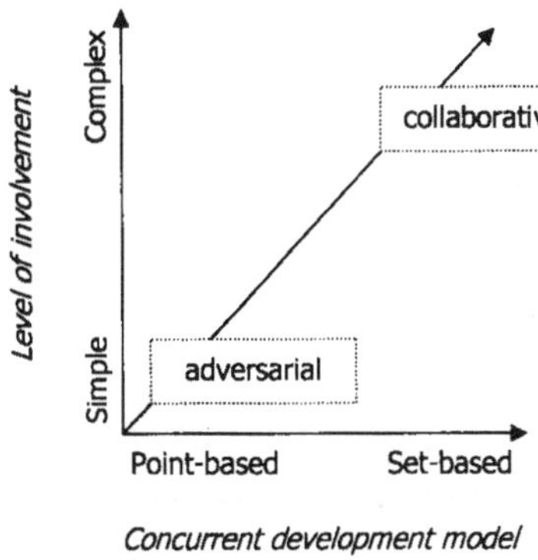

Source: adapted from Millman and Wilson (1994), own creation

Figure 28 was developed as Millman and Wilson (1994) observed key account management practices within a supply chain setting, e.g., Wal-Mart and its suppliers in retailing. Adapted to the setting of automobile development, it shows the relationship between the level of involvement described in organisational terms between the automotive company and the supplier and the use of more set-based development practices. The use of a platform architecture in the automotive development and the subsequent widening (set-based development) of the development funnel requires a wide-ranging cooperation between the automotive company and the supplier in order to achieve higher levels of integrity. This implies narrowing the set while sharing information across all participating hierarchical levels. The level of trust needed for these business processes is developed through years of intertwined practices so much that the participating companies will "succeed or fail together" (Sobek 1997, p. 38).

It is appropriate to view Figure 28 as a cooperative model, which has the economic benefit of reduced agency costs due to reduced behavioural uncertainty as the relationship develops from being adversarial to being collaborative. In fact, the three potential problems (hidden characteristics, hidden action and hidden information, and hidden intention) arising as a result of information asymmetry can be better managed from both sides as the cooperation is extended. This seems a necessary ingredient in practice in order to achieve a set-based approach in the automotive development process in cooperation with the selected supplier. Certainly, this seems to be the case in the above outline of Toyota's supplier relationships.

In particular, the problems of and possible solutions to hidden action, hidden information, and hidden intention, which all arise during a cooperation, shall be briefly discussed here.

1) Hidden action could arise when the developing company cannot properly evaluate given cost estimates from the supplier, e.g., in the course of prototype construction and testing at the supplier. Likewise a hidden information problem could arise when the developing company commissions the supplier to develop a particular module of the automobile due to the suppliers' expertise in the technology. In this case the supplier could misuse its position as an expert in the technology in order to optimize its own profit. In both cases moral hazard arises and seems to put the developing company at a disadvantage, thereby making the cooperation potentially adversarial. As mentioned this type of relationship was often observed empirically in particular at US automotive companies. This could be a reason for the relatively small supplier engineering participation at US companies observed in Figure 23.

2) Hidden intention arises when a specific irreversible investment is made, which in effect induces a dependence on the other party. In connection with the automobile development process this seems to be the case simultaneously at the developing company and at the supplier. For example the developing company can instruct the supplier to develop a particular component for the automobile development project, and the investments in tools, knowledge, etc. needed for the development cannot be applied for other potential customers. This would create a hold up problem for the supplier as he has made an irreversible investment in specific assets, which can only be used for one customer. E.g., after the irreversible specific investment the developing company could force the supplier to lower its price for the components by threatening to cancel the cooperation.

Though, the supplier can also create a hold up problem for the developing company. By refusing to cooperate the supplier could likewise make the development process become inefficient by forcing the developing company to try to find an alternative, thereby causing a negative impact on the developing company.

The above examples illustrate that there likely exists a mutual hold up situation in the cooperation between the developing company and the supplier. The extent of the hold up increases as the cooperation moves from adversarial to collaborative (see Figure 28) as the irreversible specific investments are correlated with the cooperation type. An indication of the cooperation type is for instance given by Figure 23. The relatively high percentage of supplier participation at Japanese companies indicates that they have found cooperative designs, which minimize the agency costs due to information asymmetry. In order to prevent short term opportunistic behaviour for either the developing company or the supplier, the economic viability of the cooperation depends on the established incentive structures. It can be hypothesized that the behavioural uncertainty is reduced as the cooperation becomes more established because the participating companies have both created specific irreversible investments of increasing size with time. I.e., the extent of the mutual hold up also increases with time. In addition, if the cooperation is part of a capability, which helps create a competitive advantage in the market, then the value of the cooperation would also be increasing. This is in turn would limit behavioural uncertainty by creating a win-win situation.

3.3.2 Unique Assets and Capabilities in Toyota's Development Process

Based on the above outline of Toyota's development process principles and their management of suppliers it is sensible to frame their development practices in terms of the resource-based view. As mentioned earlier, the corporate resource base is composed of assets and capabilities (competencies). The preceding sections have explained how Toyota in practice utilizes prototypes to explore the design space, sometimes in a markedly set-based fashion, and occasionally in extensive cooperation with chosen first tier suppliers. Making use of these empirical results provides the foundation for a classification of Toyota's resource base (see Table 7).

Table 7: Classification of Toyota's Resource Base

Toyota's...	
unique assets	*capabilities*
• Chief engineer	• Using prototypes to simulate production and consumption process
• Check lists	• Integrating organizational learning into checklists
• Selection matrices	• Communicating design alternatives in selection matrices
• Prototypes (production system)	• Platform development (systems engineering)
• Extensive relationships with first tier suppliers	• Developing large sets concurrently
	• Utilizing suppliers' resource base in development process
	• Knowing when to narrow the development funnel

Source: Own creation

Table 7 lists Toyota's unique assets and their capabilities, which can be identified given the empirical research undertaken predominantly on site at Toyota and in the automobile industry in general. Not all assets at Toyota contribute profoundly to their competitive advantage. Therefore Table 7 lists only the unique assets, which primarily differentiate Toyota from its competition in terms of their contribution to Toyota's competitive advantage. Also listed are the capabilities in place at Toyota. Although the listed capabilities influence Toyota's short-run competitive advantage, not all the capabilities are equally important for the sustainable (long-run) competitive advantage. As discussed earlier, it is possible to rank the capabilities. This is undertaken by making use of a framework similar to the one in Tallman and Fladmoe-Lindquist (2002) (refer also to Figure 19). Figure 29 represents a disaggregation of Toyota's competitive advantage stemming from their endowed assets and capabilities employed in the automobile development process.

Figure 29: Toyota's Capability Hierarchy

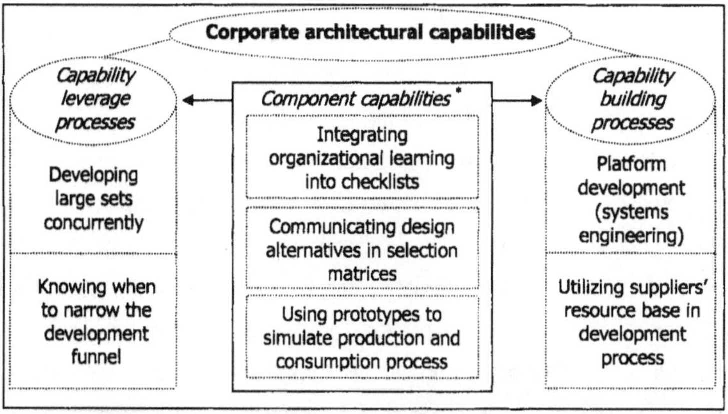

* *Note:* Toyota's assets are not depicted

Source: own creation

Figure 29 illustrates how Toyota's development process contributes to the generation of profits attributable to their component and architectural capabilities. I.e., the generation of profits is explained from the viewpoint of the strategic management literature. Figure 29 contains different levels of capabilities at Toyota (refer to Figure 19 for a description of component and architectural capabilities). It is because of these capabilities that Toyota is capable of efficiently utilizing its allocated resources. In other words, the individual capabilities and their interconnections are the reason for the efficiency gains that decisively underpin Toyota's competitive advantage. Toyota does not necessarily have the best assets in every category but rather deploys its given assets and business processes in such a way that their automobiles outperform competition regarding the CSFs in the respective target markets.

In Figure 29 the component capabilities represent the most basic level of capabilities at Toyota. They describe significantly important (for the competitive advantage) business processes, which combine Toyota's assets in a technological and organisational setting. The three component capabilities are Toyota's use of checklists, selection matrices, and prototypes respectively. The ability to represent complex engineering experiences (assets) in the form of relatively simple checklists substantially aid Toyota in storing and subsequently communicating learning inside the organisation. Likewise, the ability of Toyota to communicate design alternatives in the form of selection matrices facilitates the learning process involved in the design-build-test cycles. Particularly at the gates of the development process at Toyota the existence of meaningful selection matrices immensely aids the chief engineer in making decisions about resource allocation. The integrity of a given automobile design alternative can be seen directly in the selection matrix in terms of the relative performance results. To reiterate, the concept of selection matrices is applied within the QFD framework, and is in itself not a unique asset. Rather, it is the way in which the matrix is incorporated into the learning process of the organization, which is of importance. I.e., it is the capability to successfully apply matrices within the development process, which ultimately creates the competitive advantage. The third component capability at Toyota is the proficiency in exploiting prototypes to update the organisational information needed for the decision-making process. Although Toyota's production system is not the focus of this work, it critically underpins Toyota's capability in prototyping because prototyping can also be viewed as a manufacturing task (Clark and Fujimoto 1991). That is, the production capabilities at Toyota play an important role particularly in designing, constructing, and testing prototypes. Interestingly, due to their capability in prototyping (and consequently the resulting competitive advantage) Toyota does not outsource this task but views it as an essential component of their development system (Sobek 1997). Toyota is able to focus on prototyping as an intentional exploration of design space, in order to update the organizational information faster. This is in accordance with the view presented in Figure 5 where the development process is not only measured in technical terms but more importantly in terms of the information, which is generated with time. The net result of Toyota's capability in prototyping is a deliberate reduction of the technical uncertainty in the given design alternatives (see also Figure 9).

Toyota's component capabilities also act as "building blocks" for the highest-level (architectural) capabilities. This either occurs in Toyota's capability leveraging processes or when Toyota leverages its component capabilities in organizational learning to develop new capabilities. Toyota's capability building processes are by their nature longer term, compared to their leveraging capabilities. Capability building normally takes many years due to the double-loop learning involved and the important series of path dependent, irreversible organisational investments. The capability building processes are therefore difficult to imitate quickly. The sustainable competitive advantage and the resulting rents from the development process at Toyota are therefore primarily grounded in these architectural capabilities.

Figure 29 lists two capability leveraging processes at Toyota. These are the capability to develop large sets in parallel and the capability to manage the development process and optimally narrow the development funnel (refer also to Figure 16). These leveraging capabilities clearly benefit from the component capabilities outlined above. The capability to develop relatively large sets in parallel underlines the previously discussed advantage of exploring the design space systematically and more fully than the competition. It involves opening up the mouth of the development funnel. This capability helps prevent the learning process at Toyota become confusing and ultimately detrimental to the development effort. Toyota's component capabilities critically underpin the generation of information (prototyping capability) and subsequent storing of information and communication of design alternatives (checklist and selection matrix capabilities) needed when developing large sets concurrently. Compared to other automotive firms this seems to be a crucial capability. Clark and Fujimoto (1991) on several occasions refer to the rather quick narrowing of the development funnel at various automotive firms to be the consequence of a non-existent ability to efficiently communicate and develop sets in parallel for longer than the concept development phase. In their empirical research in the US, Liker et al. (1996, p. 177) coincide that if sets were indeed communicated, it was often due to confusion rather than a deliberate exploration of the design space on behalf of management.

Toyota's second capability leveraging process can also be illustrated in the development funnel. It involves the important task of narrowing the set of design alternatives. Only one design alternative can ultimately be implemented and the crucial process is therefore one of determining and subsequently abandoning non-optimal design alternatives. This is not an easy task. Narrowing too fast does not allow the engineers enough time to explore the design space. The potential therefore rises that management settles for an inferior design alternative. In this case the upfront investment in the automotive platform and the other design alternatives in the set can most likely not be justified from a valuation point of view. On the other hand, narrowing the development funnel too slowly epitomizes the risk of not staying within the targeted lead-time for the automobile development project. The challenge for management is in this case to avoid partially or completely missing the customers' key buying criteria as these are no longer the same as they were at the beginning of the development process. In any case, lacking capability in narrowing the development funnel is aggravated by the existence of technical and market uncertainty. If uncertainty is high then it is probably important for management to explore different design alternatives and for them to make sure that they have at least one design alternative, which meets customer buying criteria. As mentioned previously, at Toyota the chief engineering is responsible for narrowing the development funnel. He therefore is a unique asset for Toyota. Toyota clearly places much emphasis on training and selecting chief engineers, as the capability to narrow the development funnel without the chief engineer would be severely limited. Unfortunately, in the literature there is no outline of the principles by which the chief engineer exercises his flexibility in narrowing the set. Chapter 4 of this work shall present a formal model, which, based on company information and market prices, is capable of producing value-optimizing recommendations.

The other types of architectural capabilities are the capability building processes. These capabilities most likely contribute to longer run efficiency gains as they per definition precede other capabilities. It is possible to identify two capability building processes at

Toyota. These are the platform development capability and the capability to utilize the suppliers' resource base in the development process. Both are concerned with providing a basis for other capabilities and continuously exercising managerial flexibility to address a changing internal and external environment. I.e., the architectural capabilities at Toyota are highly integrated with organizational learning. Toyota is not only focused on managing the development funnel (single-loop learning), but they are also focussed on changing the way they manage (meta-learning) the development funnel. As Toyota is on the leading-edge within the automobile industry when it comes to set-based development, they clearly have some sort of meta-learning ability in exercising their flexibility optimally to deal with uncertainty.

1) The first architectural capability, which can be identified at Toyota, is an ability to do systems engineering (platform development). This capability precedes the individual automobile development project. The systems engineering capability at Toyota is concerned with designing optimal platforms for the complete current und future portfolio of automotive products. As was discussed preciously, a set-based development process implicitly assumes a modular product design (see, e.g., Figure 15). Only with given technical design standards for the product interfaces can an automotive company switch between alternative designs. Though, the flexibility to choose between alternative designs in parallel is probably worth little if the interfaces are designed poorly. In this case the automotive company can choose only between one alternative with low integrity and other equally mediocre alternatives. The end result is an automobile with low integrity. The systems engineering capability is therefore an architectural capability because it helps pave the way at Toyota for a set-based development process. Without it Toyota would be forced to develop generally in a more point-based manner.

2) The second architectural capability at Toyota is the ability to efficiently utilize the resource base of select first tier suppliers. In the literature Toyota's model of supplier relationships has become a benchmark for the automobile industry (refer in general to Hagel and Brown 2005). Toyota understands better than the competition how to build up and maintain win-win relationships with suppliers. This allows Toyota to choose

where to build competence leadership (compare with Prahalad and Hamel 1990). Sobek (1997) observed that Toyota has chosen to specialize primarily in engines and electrical systems. In these subsystems Toyota relies solely on their own engineering capabilities and does not involve suppliers in developing them. In this case electrical systems form an essential part of the platform design, and Toyota therefore chooses to keep control of these capabilities in-house. In other words, Toyota is a network integrator. As discussed previously, this is a precondition for an economically sensible network relationship in that Toyota does not loose control of its architectural capabilities.

There are two benefits for Toyota of working closely (organisationally) with select formidable suppliers.

1) First, due to Toyota's unique relationship with suppliers, Toyota can leverage their resource base directly into a current automotive development project. This allows Toyota to drastically widen the development funnel with little or no incurred upfront marginal investment costs. The supplier has potentially specialized in a given subsystem or component as a result of the suppliers' unique path-dependant series of irreversible investments in their key technologies and learning. Because Toyota possesses a capability in working closely with their suppliers, Toyota can access their suppliers' organisational information base to a greater extent (compared to an adversarial supplier relationship). E.g., in a complex organisational involvement with a supplier (see Figure 28) an engineer at the supplier is more likely to pick up the phone and discuss openly with an engineer at Toyota the trade-offs between various design alternatives. As long as the automotive competition cannot duplicate this type of relationship with the same supplier, they have in practice only limited access to the supplier. Therefore, Toyota has in effect created a barrier to entry to its supplier network.

2) The second advantage resulting from Toyota's capability to work with suppliers is related to Toyota's long-run competitive position. By working closely with competent suppliers Toyota is able to learn about new and potentially valuable technologies earlier than the competition. This is a type of Bayesian learning (see, e.g., Jackson, Kalai, and Smorodinsky 1999 for an overview). This in turn implies that suppliers' capabilities are getting into the core operating processes of the business at Toyota (Hagel and Brown

2005). That is, the effective boundary of the firm has moved closer to the architectural capabilities. Utilizing the suppliers' capabilities allows Toyota to exercise its managerial flexibility to adapt its architectural capabilities to the new environment. Toyota thereby ensures a continued role as a network orchestrator. E.g., Toyota could choose to optimize their platform design to increase the integrity of future automobiles. Toyota's supplier capability is most likely a key value driver in Toyota's development process, and the value hereof shall be explored in more detail in chapter 5.

3.4 Chapter Summary

This chapter dealt with how an organization attains a competitive advantage. The literature proposes two main groups of models to solve this problem: strategic fit and strategic stretch. The first group, industry structural analysis, focuses primarily on the external environment of the organization and *where* the organization should choose to compete. The second group, RBV, focuses mainly on the internal environment of the organization and *how* the organization should choose to compete.

The central tenet of the RBV is that an organization achieves Ricardian[37] rents resulting from market imperfections due to firm-level efficiency advantage(s) in meeting the CSFs better than the competition. There exist two components of this efficiency advantage: resources and capabilities. Both are unique and cannot be copied or acquired easily by the competition, thereby fortifying the advantage.

Of particular importance are the capabilities because they represent complex knowledge resources. As was also the case in chapter 2, information is at the core of the process of sequential choice. An organization's potential to apply and develop its capabilities is determined by its absorptive capacity, which determines how the organization learns. The most basic form of learning is single-loop learning and occurs when an organization exercises its flexibility. The more advanced form of learning is labelled double-loop learning and takes place when an organization learns about the way it learns. Double-loop learning therefore implies a compounding effect in the process of sequential choice.

[37] Due to the superior quality of the organization's factor inputs (in this case resources and capabilities).

It is purposeful to classify capabilities according to two categories: component capabilities and architectural capabilities. Component capabilities are individual firm-specific business processes. Architectural capabilities employ and develop the component capabilities. I.e., architectural capabilities have a platform property, which can also be utilized in working with suppliers in order to gain access to their capabilities. Consequently, the RBV views resources as the building blocks of component capabilities, and component capabilities as the building blocks of architectural capabilities.

Based on empirical research undertaken in the automobile industry, it is possible to identify two archetypes of automotive development processes. The first archetype has a focused mouth and practices a fast narrowing of the development funnel. This system may be considered a derivative of the point-based concurrent development process. It is observed frequently in the US and Europe. The focus is on technical aspects of the prototype developed. The development process is traditionally functional in nature and results in lower degrees of internal and external integration. The second archetype has a wide mouth and carries out a slow narrowing of the development funnel. This system may be considered a derivative of the set-based concurrent development process. It is observed frequently in Japan. The focus is on the prototype as an information-generating vehicle to be utilized as part of the organizational learning process. The development process is typically cross-functional in nature and results in higher degrees of internal and external integration.

The empirical results therefore raise the issue of whether an automotive developer can achieve a competitive advantage through the use of a wider development funnel, i.e., by increasing the set of design alternatives being developed concurrently. An important aspect of widening the development funnel was the observed use of suppliers in the early stages of the development process. This was especially the case in Japan and at Toyota in particular.

Finally, the automotive development process at Toyota was considered as being representative of the set-based approach and analysed in detail. Based upon the empirical research undertaken at Toyota in Japan it was possible to identify several unique resources and capabilities as applied within Toyota's development process. The capabilities were subsequently ranked, and the result was the identification of three component capabilities as well as four architectural capabilities.

Chapter 4: Real Option Model of the Automotive Development Process

The purpose of this chapter is to deal mainly with answering subproblem 3 of the problem statement:
What are the relevant real options available to management in the development process, and how are these valued from the perspective of the developing company?

The overall purpose of this chapter is to present a general valuation model for the automobile development process. This will be done by further developing the insights presented in the previous chapters in order to construct a quantitative valuation model, with which the automobile development process can be valued from the viewpoint of the automotive company's ownership.
The chapter is outlined as follows. The first part contends with the role of financial markets as an objective arbiter on the value of corporate strategy. The underlying rationale is one of identifying and applying the opportunity cost of the invested resources in the development process to determine an optimal development process setup. The second part presents a general valuation framework for all types of claims. In complete markets the objective is to determine the price, which investors would pay for a given automobile development process setup. Particular emphasis is given to valuation models assuming incomplete markets. Here the objective is to determine the interval of valid prices, which investors would pay for a given automobile development process setup. The third part deals with option valuation and discusses the real options inherent in the automotive development process. Firm level efficiency advantages within the development process are to be identified and valued using valuation models, which are able to capture the resulting asymmetric payoff structures. The fourth part develops a valuation model for the real option to switch in order to solve quantitatively for the optimal automobile development process setup.

4.1 The Role and Structure of Financial Markets

The concept of the market plays a crucial role in financial economics. The view taken here is that this importance can also be extended to the area of strategy and the automobile development process in particular.

4.1.1 The Discipline of Financial Markets

Asset prices in the financial markets contain information about return and risk (e.g., the market price of risk, see equation (4.20)) and present an important input to any development process. The market helps decision-makers allocate resources to various design alternatives by acting as a benchmark for performance. Amram and Kulatilaka (1999, p. 95) state that managers: "can incorporate the market's objective measures of value under uncertainty into their own strategic choices." In order to apply this "discipline of the markets" (Amram and Kulatilaka 1999, p. 95) managers must seek to incorporate the market's information about prices assigned to various states of the world. E.g., in developing an engine for an automobile the value of the engine can be deduced in part from the market's information regarding future gas prices. Management could calculate the volatility of long term oil contracts in the futures and options markets to get an estimate. This volatility estimate derived from the markets could then be applied in the internal forecasts of future purchasing behaviour of the automobile, which in turn can be utilized to calculate the expected FCFs and thereby market value resulting from the engine design. An important evaluation of the economic viability of the engine design is in this manner supplied by the markets. The role of the financial markets is therefore to help management value the range of available corporate strategies at any given point in time to the best interest of owners.

Once management has found the value of the object in question it is possible to apply a recursive method in order to deduce the optimal set of strategic choices. As the size and timing of cash flows are the basis for any valuation, management can now focus on the choices, and thereby strategy, leading to the envisioned cash flows. Therefore, implicit in any valuation is the optimal decision-making process, which leads to the mentioned cash flows. It is this optimal strategy, which is ultimately of interest when discussing the managerial applications of this work. The financial markets consequently contain information and direction for the corporate decision-making process.

4.1.2 Separating the Investment and Financing Decisions

An important assumption underlying this market discipline is the separation of the owners' investment and financing preferences. This is the so-called Fisher separation theorem to complete markets (Fisher 1930; and Copeland, Weston, and Shastri 2005). By maximizing the total present value of the FCFs associated with a given automotive development strategy, management is automatically acting in the best interest of the company ownership. The financial markets therefore unite investors with differing preferences regarding the timing and size of investment and consumption (Trigeorgis 2000, p. 26). I.e., the market rate functions as an equilibrium mechanism. Under ideal circumstances (complete and perfect markets) the valuation of the automotive development process can in practice be simplified to a great extent by focusing primarily on the financial markets for guidance in the process of corporate resource allocation. Though, in a strict sense, financial markets are in practice seldom perfect and complete, which in turn imposes limits to the market discipline. These cases will be discussed later on.

4.1.3 Financial Economics, Free Cash Flows, and Strategic Management

The automotive development process has until now been cast as a subcomponent of the overall strategy followed by the automotive company. Therefore, in order to value various setups of the development process, it is necessary at the outset to have some form of conversion from a largely qualitative framework (strategic management) to a quantitative one (financial economics). Traditionally this interface is described in terms of FCFs (see, e.g., Myers 1984). In other words, only the nature and structure of cash flows serve as an input to the following valuation models. First, the automotive development process must therefore be viewed as a sequential decision-making process resulting in a series of cash flows, which in turn are applied in a valuation model. Second, not only the stand-alone expected cash flows are of importance for the valuation but also the information, which management expects to learn about the distribution of these cash flows (see, e.g., Bernado and Chowdry 2001, p. 212). That is, the automotive development process must be viewed also as an information generating process (see Figure 5). There is a strong parallel here to the concept of a filtration as applied in financial mathematics (see, e.g., Duffie 1996, p. 272; a filtration is defined in chapter 4.2.1). It is the sequential disclosure of the information set, which drives financial market prices. Likewise information about cash flows ensuing from the automotive development process has a value and should play an essential role in the valuation of the development process.

Based on the above outline it is thus possible to mirror the automotive development process (an elemental part of strategic management) in the financial markets (Borison 2003). The view taken here is that strategy and finance describe two sides of the same coin. Indeed, Myers (1984, p. 130) states that: "Finance theory and strategic planning can be viewed as two cultures looking at the same problem." This is the perspective underlying Figure 31. It shows how the automobile development process can be both analyzed in strategic terms as wells as valued in the light of financial market prices. This is accomplished by specifically valuing the component and architectural capabilities identified in Toyota's development process. The fundamental idea is that valuation of technology development is focused on valuing linkages. Boer (1998, p. 46) notes that: "Valuing technology is all about valuing linkages." Indeed, capabilities are valuable because they link other business processes and assets with each other in an uncertain environment. That is, there is a conscious exercise of managerial flexibility underlying capabilities (see, e.g., Kogut and Kulatilaka 2001).

4.1.4 Capabilities and Real Options

In finance, the pendant to a capability is a real option. It embodies the "'economizing' of organizational intuition" (Bowman and Hurry 1993, p. 777). Historically, the term "real options" was mentioned the first time by Myers (1977) referring to managerial flexibilities in research and development and manufacturing plants. In the 1980s the first academic articles on the topic of real options showed up, such as the ones by McDonald and Siegel (1986), Trigeorgis and Mason (1987), and Dixit (1989). In 1994 the first textbook on the topic of real option valuation by Dixit and Pindyck (1994) followed. Within the last 10 years the subject of real options has become commonplace in the academic finance literature such as, e.g., in the standard finance textbook Brealey, Myers, and Allen (2005).

The real option framework provides the insights needed to explain the RBV from a financial markets perspective. As Peteraf and Barney (2003, p. 309) note: "it is essential to understand the limits to the domain of RBT. Unless RBT is understood as a resource-level and efficiency-oriented analytical tool, its contribution cannot be understood and appreciated fully." The basic line of argumentation in this work is to employ the real options framework to enlighten the efficiency-based view of the corporation encompassed in the RBV. Kogut and Kulatilaka (2001, p. 745) define a real option as an "investment in physical and human assets that provides [management with] the opportunity to respond to future contingent events." Real options represent a taxonomy of intangible resources and capabilities (Hall 1993, p. 607). As with corporate resources (assets and capabilities), real options are also characterized by uncertainty, flexibility, and irreversibility (Dixit and Pindyck 1994). Real options, analogue to financial options, derive their value from a combination of one or more risky underlying variables and managerial flexibility to adapt the corporate strategy accordingly. Consequently real options curve the downside risk of the cash flow distribution and additionally extend the upside potential of the cash flow distribution (Trigeorgis 2000). Real options are therefore able to capture the effect of the asymmetric payoff structures (see also Pandza et al. 2003, pp. 1016-1017) identified in the automobile development process and shall be the preferred instrument for modelling it.

In the same way as strategic management, real options are instrumental in giving normative prescriptions to corporate resource allocation. Real options can help management think of corporate strategy not as a "'portfolio of businesses' but as a 'portfolio of initiatives'" (Bryan 2002, p. 19). In other words, business strategies can be modelled as "chains of real options" (Luehrman 1998, p. 90). Real options provide a good opportunity for analyzing the corporate resource base from the viewpoint of shareholders. Bowman and Hurry (1993, p. 762) characterize real options as arising from "the interplay of the organization's existing investments, its knowledge and capacities, and its environmental opportunities." They can therefore be utilized to identify valuable applications (strategic stretch) of the corporate resources to "white spaces" (Kogut and Kulatilaka 2001, p. 744) in the market topography.

Having explained the traits of both capabilities and real options, it is now purposeful to take a more extensive view on the role of information in relation to capabilities and real options. Of particular importance are the capabilities because they represent complex knowledge resources. As was also the case in chapter 2, information is at the core of the process of sequential choice. An organization's potential to apply and develop its capabilities is determined by its absorptive capacity, which determines how the organization learns. The most basic form of learning is single-loop learning and occurs when an organization exercises its flexibility, i.e., when an organization exercises a single real option. The more advanced form of learning is labelled double-loop learning and takes place when an organization learns about the way it learns. Double-loop learning therefore implies a compounding effect in the process of sequential choice, i.e., when an organization exercises a compound real option.

The above outline makes it is possible to value an entity (e.g., company, business project, development process, etc.) as the sum of its asset in place plus its capabilities (see, e.g., Myers 1984).

$$\text{ENPV} = -I_0 + \text{PV}(\text{FCF}) + \text{Real Option(s)}$$

(4.1) $$\Updownarrow$$

$$\text{Value of automotive development process} = \text{Assets} + \text{Capabilities}$$

Equation (4.1) is the most basic valuation equation for the automotive development process as it shall be applied in this thesis. It partly mirrors equation (2.2) and furthermore shows the parallel to the strategic management framework. Equation (4.1) states that the value of a given automotive development process is the sum of the value of the assets in place plus the value of the firm-specific capabilities. In terms of financial economics the assets in place represent the value of the automobile if management stays with the original plan and exercises no flexibility to shape the FCFs once uncertainties have been revealed. The real option(s) component represents the incremental value of managerial action to shape the FCFs because the internal and external environments are uncertain and make managerial deviations from the original plan valuable. Management should therefore aim to maximize the value of their automotive development process by identifying the combination of assets and capabilities, which yield the highest ENPV.

Even though strategic management and real options obviously share many traits, there are some differences. Apart from the obvious difference in modelling (qualitative models compared to quantitative models) strategic management is basically focused on "an open systems" approach whereas the real options approach takes place in "closed system" where choice becomes a logical operation (Pandza et al. 2003, p. 1012). When applying a quantitative valuation model to a complex, ambiguous and sometimes paradoxical nature of organizational capabilities, validity automatically becomes an issue.[38] In particular, there are clear limitations to a real options model of the automotive development process due to the different types of uncertainty resolution in strategic management and a real options model respectively. E.g., Adner and Levinthal (2004, pp. 77-78) state: "The importance of organizational factors in determining the applicability of options logic increases as real options theory is extended from the evaluation of investments in physical assets, for which the resolution of uncertainty is exogenous to firm action and the scope of possible firm response to this uncertainty is relatively constrained ..., to the evaluation of investments in strategic opportunities, for which the resolution of uncertainty is largely endogenous to firm action, and the scope

[38] This matter was envisioned already in chapter 1 where the reliability and validity of the thesis was discussed.

for possible modifications in the initial initiative is vast." Concerning the applicability of the real options framework to the automobile development process, however, the real option model of the automobile development process has a very high degree of reliability due to the analogy with the before mentioned capabilities underlying the management of the automobile development process. Thus the approach taken here is to state the assumptions for the real option model in a clear and unambiguous manner, concentrating primarily on a discussion of the model results.

4.2 General Asset Valuation

An important part of real options is the valuation process, which builds on a quantitative model setup. The following sections are devoted to establishing a brief theoretical base for asset valuation in general and for options in particular. In particular, the field of financial economics deals with most of the models and assumptions to be introduced. The ensuing insights represent the basic financial market and valuation principles of most standard textbooks on financial economics and function as a framework for the quantitative valuation model of the development process, which will be utilized later on.
In finance, valuation is involved with comparing a specific asset to other marketed assets. Valuation is "the common idea of finding a comparable marketed asset when pricing a new one" (Luenberger 2001, p. 2). It is therefore meaningful to present a model of the financial markets, which will serve as a reference point for the valuation.

4.2.1 A Multiperiod Securities Market Model

The following section draws upon basic insights from most standard textbooks on financial mathematics such as, e.g., Duffie (1996) and Bingham and Kiesel (2004). Due to the multiperiod setting of the automotive development process, a multiperiod securities market model shall be the starting point. For the sake of convenience a discrete-time state approach is chosen. With appropriate changes, the following models and concepts also hold in a continuous-time state-space setting. Though, the discrete-time state-space is more fitting for the valuation setup to be applied in this thesis because of the numerical approximation method to be applied in chapter 4.4.

There are $T+1$ trading dates (t) with $t = 0,1,...,T$. For each point in time t there are K possible states of nature (ω). The set of ω make up the sample space (Ω) with $\Omega = \{\omega_1, \omega_2, ..., \omega_K\}$. The sample space therefore refers to the set of possible scenarios at any given point in time and graphically can be drawn as a grid of points in time and state space. P is the probability measure and is defined on Ω with $P(\omega)$ being the probability that a given state ω will be reached for all $\omega \in \Omega$. P totally describes the set of possible states at the next point in time, i.e., $\Sigma_{\omega\in\Omega} P(\omega) = 1$. The way price-relevant information is disclosed to the market participants with time is a filtration (F_t) (e.g., Duffie 1996, p. 21). This information is a necessary input to any pricing problem. F_t represents a nested sequence of information, so market participants have complete knowledge of past and current prices of the N risky assets.[39] This is also congruent with the weak level of market efficiency. There is a risk-free bond (B_t) in the market place with

(4.2) $$R_F \equiv {(B_t - B_{t-1})}\big/{B_{t-1}} \geq 0$$

being the risk-free interest rate from time t-1 to t (e.g., Duffie 1996, p. 12). Finally, at any given state ω and point in time t there are N risky assets

(4.3) $$S_i(t,\omega) \quad \text{for } 1 \leq i \leq N$$

in the market, each following a diffusion process. As only price-relevant information flows into the valuation of $S_i(t,\omega)$, the risky assets are adapted to the information in F_t. Because new information is per definition random the price movements of $S_i(t,\omega)$ are consequently also random. This insight is also known as Samuelson's Proof (Samuelson 1965). With regard to the automobile development process, the N risky assets function as important inputs to the valuation of the automobile development process because

[39] Formally, the N risky assets form a subspace (time t and state ω) of a so-called "Hilbert space" (see, e.g., Luenberger 2001, p. 5; and Bingham and Kiesel 2004, p. 308).

they contain information about risk and return. This is the above-mentioned market discipline.

4.2.2 No Arbitrage Condition

An important feature of the prices of the marketed assets is the absence of arbitrage. Smith and McCardle (1998, p. 201) state: a "decision maker cannot make profits without investing some money or taking some risks: there is no 'easy money' to be made in securities trading". An arbitrage (e.g., Duffie 1996, p. 3) is given by the following three conditions such that

i) $V_0 = 0$
ii) $V_1 \geq 0$, and
ii) $E[V_1] > 0$.

V_0 and V_1 symbolize the value of a portfolio at times 0 and 1 respectively. The first condition states that an arbitrageur has created a portfolio with 0 costs at time 0. The second condition implies that the value of the portfolio at time 1 is non-negative. The final condition means that the created portfolio has a strictly positive expected value at time 1. If the above three conditions are met, an investor can generate a profit without any risk of loss, i.e., a riskless profit. Assuming that all investors have equal access to the markets (perfect market assumption) they would immediately create a trading strategy in order to take advantage of the pricing inconsistencies. Through the forces of supply and demand asset prices would inevitably move into equilibrium, thereby eliminating any arbitrage opportunity. For any valuation model to be reasonable arbitrage must therefore be absent.

4.2.3 Equivalent Martingale Measure

As explained above, the probability measure determines the movements of $S_i(t,\omega)$ from one point in time to the next point in time. The real-world probability function for asset price returns is given by P as described above. For particular valuation problems (e.g., valuing contingent claims) it can be convenient to change the probability measure into a so-called "equivalent martingale" (or similarly "risk-neutral") measure Q (see, e.g., Duffie 1996, p. 28). To begin with, a definition of a martingale is needed. A stochastic variable Z_t is said to be a martingale if

(4.4) $E\left[Z_{t+s}|F_t\right]=Z_t$, for all $s,t\geq 0$.

That is, the expected growth rate of Z_t is 0. Under the real world probability measure *P*, market participants expect a positive growth rate of assets, and these stochastic processes are called submartingales given by

(4.5) $E\left[Z_{t+s}|F_t\right]>Z_t$, for all $s,t\geq 0$

or equivalently

(4.6) $E_P\left[Z_{t+s}|F_t\right]>Z_t$, for all $s,t\geq 0$

to denote that the expectation is taken with respect to the real-world probability measure *P*. Rephrasing equation (4.6) in terms of a risky asset $S_i(t)$, one gets

(4.7) $E_P\left[S_i(t+s)|F_t\right]>S_i(t)$, for all $s,t\geq 0$.

It is now possible to change the probability measure from *P* (real-world) to *Q* (risk-neutral), thereby transforming the submartingale in equation (4.7) into a martingale. To start with, let $S_i^*(t)$ denote a discounted price process (e.g., Duffie 1996, p.29) given by

(4.8) $S_i^*(t)\equiv {S_i(t)}/{B_t}$.

It can be shown that

(4.9) $E_Q\left[\Delta S_i^*(t+1)|F_t\right]=0$ for $i=1,\dots,N$.

As is the case under the real-world probability measure *P*, the probabilities under *Q* must also sum to 1, i.e., $\Sigma_{\omega\in\Omega}Q(\omega)=1$. If the expected change in S_i is 0 then the following equation must be true:

(4.10) $$E_Q\left[S_i^*(t+s)\middle|F_t\right]=S_i^*(t).$$

By changing to the risk-neutral probability measure Q the discounted value (using a risk-free bond in equation (4.2) as a state-price deflator) of the risky asset S_i can be seen to have 0 growth. In other words, in the risk-neutral world (due to the probability measure Q) assets can be seen to be growing at a rate equal to the risk-free rate. This is an important result in the valuation of risky assets and can also be applied to e.g., contingent claims (such as options) in order to value asymmetric payoffs in the automobile development process. This will be emphasized in the following sections.

4.2.4 Lattice of Asset Price Movements - The Binomial Tree

Equations (4.4)-(4.10) are general results. Still, in order to value a contingent claim on the risky asset, it is necessary to make further assumptions regarding its stochastic price process. In the following, the binomial model (Cox et al. 1979) for asset price movements shall be presented.[40] In each time period, the risky asset S_i can move either up or down (hence the name binomial) by constant factors u or d respectively. The following restrictions are made to u and d: $0<d<1<u$, and in order for the binomial process to be recombining u and d are inversely related with

(4.11) $$u=\frac{1}{d}\Leftrightarrow ud=1.$$

Further, the real-world probability that S_i will move up equals p with $0<p<1$. Equivalently the probability for a downward move by S_i is 1-p. The factors u, d, and p are constant for every time period. The ω attainable states for S_i at time t (i.e., $S_i(t)$) are given by

[40] In the limit the binomial model approximates the well-known geometric Brownian motion, a subgroup of Ito processes. This is ensured by matching the expected mean and standard deviation of discrete-time stochastic process with the continuous-time stochastic process, an approach shared with lattice methods (refer to Figure 30) in general. (see, e.g., Hull 2003)

(4.12) $$S(t,\omega) = S(0,\omega)u^n d^{t-n} \text{ for } \omega \in \Omega$$

where n is the number of upward moves taken by S from time 0 to time t. Likewise it is possible to specify the probability (P_P) that $S_i(t,\omega)$ will be reached to be

(4.13) $$P_P\left[S_i(t,\omega) = S_i(0,\omega)u^n d^{t-n}\right] = \binom{t}{n} p^n (1-p)^{t-n}, \; n = 0,1,\ldots,t.$$

In equation (4.13) $p^n(1-p)^{t-n}$ is the real-world probability measure P. $\binom{t}{n}$ is the so-called binomial coefficient. Because the stochastic price process for S_i is recombining the binomial coefficient specifies the number of possible paths, which S_i can take to reach state $S_i(t,\omega)$. As seen in equations (4.7) and (4.9) it is possible to change the probability measure from the real-world P to the risk-neutral Q. Assuming a constant risk-free interest rate (R_F) the martingale measure for the binomial model is given by

(4.14) $$Q(\omega) = q^n(1-q)^{t-n}, \text{ with } q = \frac{(1+R_F)-d}{u-d} \text{ and } 0 < q < 1.$$

Under the martingale measure Q the probability (P_Q) of reaching state $S_i(t,\omega)$ becomes

(4.15) $$P_Q\left[S_i(t,\omega) = S_i(0,\omega)u^n d^{t-n}\right] = \binom{t}{n} q^n (1-q)^{t-n}, \; n = 0,1,\ldots,t.$$

Using the probability measure Q provided in equation (4.14) one can replicate the result in equation (4.10) for the approximating stochastic process in the binomial model. The outcome is

(4.16) $$\begin{gathered} E_Q\left[S_i^*(t+1)\middle|S_i^*(t)\right] = \\ \left(S_i^*(t)/(1+R_F)\right)\left[\frac{1+R_F-d}{u-d}u + \frac{u-1-R_F}{u-d}d\right] = S_i^*(t) \end{gathered}$$

The risky asset can be shown to be a martingale under the risk-neutral probability measure. The risky asset S_i therefore also grows at the risk-free rate in the risk-neutral world when the binomial model is employed. Compared to equation (4.10) the conditional expectation in equation (4.16) is stated in terms of the current price of the risky asset and not F_t. This is because the binomial model is derived using the Markov property, which states that only the current price of the risky asset is relevant for the expected future price. I.e., the specific path followed by S_i until now is not of importance. Note that the above binomial model assumes constant *u, d,* and *p.* That is, the Markov chain is stationary.

4.2.5 Complete Markets – Spanning and Equilibrium Pricing Models

A final characteristic of financial markets, which shall be discussed here, is market completeness. A very important part of any valuation model is the fundamental assumption regarding the degree of market completeness. Valuation and the degree of market completeness are intrinsically linked. A market is complete if any claim can be replicated (valued) using a trading strategy consisting of other marketed assets. That is, a replicating portfolio is created, which exactly mirrors the payoffs of the claim across all states $\omega \in \Omega$. If the market is complete the claim is said to be attainable, and the value of the claim is the weighted sum of its payoffs in the various states ω timed with the so-called state prices (see equation (4.18) for the respective states). In order to identify the state prices, let $X(\omega)$ be a pure-state-claim (see Arrow and Debreu 1954) given by

$$\textbf{(4.17)} \qquad X(\omega) = \begin{cases} 1, & \omega = \hat{\omega} \\ 0, & \omega \neq \hat{\omega} \end{cases}$$

$X(\omega)$ only has a payoff of 1 in the state(s) $\hat{\omega}$, and for the other states it has a 0 payoff. The discounted value of this claim is labelled the state price (ψ; see, e.g., Duffie 1996, p. 68) for state $\hat{\omega}$ given by

$$\textbf{(4.18)} \qquad E_Q[X / B_1] = \sum_{\omega} Q(\omega) X(\omega) / B_1(\omega) = Q(\hat{\omega}) / B_1(\hat{\omega}) = \psi(\hat{\omega})$$

Given the risk-free bond B and the risk-free interest rate R_F the state price is simply the risk-neutral probability $Q(\hat{\omega})$ of reaching the payoff state(s) $\hat{\omega}$ discounted with the risk-free rate (embedded in $B_1 = B_0(1+R_F)$; see also equation (4.2)). This result can be generalized to the valuation of marketed assets in general. The arbitrage-free value of any marketed asset (S_i) can be found to be the probability-weighted sum of the asset dividends (DIV) in every possible state (ω) under the martingale measure discounted at the risk-free rate (e.g., Duffie 1996, p. 69). This is conveyed in equation (4.19).

(4.19) $$S_i = \sum_{\omega=1}^{K} DIV_i(\omega)\psi(\omega) \text{ , where } DIV_i(\omega) = \{DIV(1), DIV(2), \ldots, DIV(K)\}$$

In the literature this approach is formally called spanning (Luenberger 2001) or Contingent Claims Analysis (CCA) in the case of option valuation (see, e.g., Dixit and Pindyck 1994 for an outline of this approach in valuing real options) and entails a linear combination of marketed assets. It is convenient to directly employ the state prices (see equation (4.18) as the most basic prices of the various states. In this way the value of the claim is consistent with existing marketed assets. Specifically "...the value obtained from a CCA model has the advantage of being consistent with an equilibrium price structure." (Kamrad 1995, p. 142).[41] Spanning does not assume any type of risk-preference on the behalf of investors, making it convenient for pricing assets. When spanning is possible it can be shown that there is one unique probability measure Q (see, e.g., Trigeorgis 2000, p. 16).

There is a second group of valuation models in finance. These are the so-called equilibrium models.[42] One such model is the Capital Asset Pricing Model (CAPM) (refer to Sharpe 1964 and Lintner 1965). It states that the expected return on an asset is

---

[41] In the case of the automotive development process the projected cash flows ($DIV_i(\omega)$) from an automotive development process are priced directly by the market equilibrium prices ($\psi(\omega)$). This is the implication of the above-mentioned market discipline and is seen clearly in equation (4.19).

[42] The equilibrium valuation models are referred to as "absolute valuation models" by Garman (1976, p. 2). On the other hand the "relative" valuation models are given by equation (4.19) and imply some form of spanning.

composed of the risk-free rate plus a risk-premium depending on the amount of risk in the asset (see equation (4.20) and, e.g., Duffie 1996, p. 12).

(4.20) $$E[R_i] = R_F + \frac{E[R_M] - R_F}{\sigma_M^2} \operatorname{cov}(R_M, R_i)$$

where

R_i = return on asset i
R_M = return on market portfolio
R_F = return on risk-free bond
σ_m^2 = variance of the rate of return on the market portfolio
cov = covariance

This type of pricing assets implies that investors are averse to risk (quadratic utility function). In order to assume risk, investors require a risk-premium, which consists of the amount of risk ($\operatorname{cov}(R_M, R_i)$) in the given asset, times the market price of risk (Duffie 1996, pp. 109-111)

(4.21) $$\text{Market Price of Risk} = \lambda = \left(E[R_M] - R_F\right)/\sigma_M^2,$$

which is the extra return granted by the market for each unit of risk in the asset. In other words, investors are only rewarded for carrying systematic risk (average portfolio covariances in a large portfolio). The underlying assumption for this is that investors are presumed to be invested in broad portfolios. As the number of assets in a portfolio increase the only remaining risk is the average covariances (see, e.g., Brealey and Myers 2005).

Cox and Ross (1976), Garman (1976), and Harrison and Kreps (1979) showed that there is an interesting link between the real-world and risk-neutral probability measures outlined above. In fact λ plays the role of helping transform the valuation of contingent claims from taking place under the probability measure P to being valued under Q (see, e.g., Garman 1976, p. 28). Hull and White (1990) also utilize this approach in order to derive a trinomial lattice for derivatives valuation. I.e., it is possible to subtract the risk premium (equal to $\lambda_i \bullet \sigma_i$) from the expected return on the underlying asset in order to reduce the real-world drift to the risk-free rate (see equation (4.22)).

(4.22) $\mu_i - \lambda_i\sigma_i = r$ where σ_i = the volatility of the return on asset i

This allows the use of the martingale measure (see equation (4.10)) and risk-neutral valuation principles in general. An example of this approach is given by Cox, Ingersoll, and Ross (1985).[43] Kulatilaka (1993) also utilizes the approach to value an industrial steam boiler.

Of interest in this thesis is the assumption in the CAPM regarding the degree of market completeness. As it is an equilibrium model it is derived, among other things, using all assets in order to find the equilibrium pricing kernel. If the market is complete it is possible to value e.g., the real options in the automobile development process using an equilibrium approach. Because the CAPM presumes risk-averse investors the contingent claims must be valued employing the continuously adjusted risk-adjusted discount rate as prescribed by the equilibrium model (Kamrad 1995, p. 141). This corresponds to the so-called "Dynamic Programming" (DP) approach as applied to the valuation of real options by Dixit and Pindyck (1994). A principle challenge with this method is to find the appropriate discount rate (Fama 1996). This task is made harder by the fact that the options involved in practice change the risk characteristics of the project. Still, it can be shown that CCA and DP give identical results when markets are complete (Dixit and Pindyck 1994). Examples of the equilibrium approach are also found in Childs, Ott, and Triantis (1998) and Childs and Triantis (1999). They set out to value the real options in a development process by assuming that the development process does not change the equilibrium pricing kernel. That is, the development process does not expand the investor's opportunity set, and accordingly the equilibrium pricing kernel stays intact.

---

[43] Likewise, when markets are complete it is possible to derive option-pricing formulas assuming risk-aversion instead of risk-neutrality, see, e.g., Rubenstein (1976).

4.2.6 Incomplete Markets – Partial Spanning Models

If the market is incomplete (or equivalently partially complete) there are one or more claims, which are not attainable. In other words, it is no longer possible to value a claim W in terms of existing marketed assets because it is not in the span of the basic assets (see, e.g., Luenberger 2002). I.e., the there are so-called private risks in a given claim, W, producing a payoff vector with more dimensions than the market subspace (see, e.g., Ng and Bjornsson 2001, p. 5). These private risks per definition provide no information about the future market priced states (ω) of the world. In other words, information about private risks is not in F_t, which contains only information as represented by the marketed asset states $\omega \in \Omega$ (Smith and Nau 1995, p. 808). In the case of incomplete markets the marketed assets do not fully contain information about return and risk for the claim W to be uniquely priced (in terms of market prices).

In most real option applications in practice there is little evidence of complete markets. Indeed, a promising field of real option valuation methods in practice is the case of incomplete markets (see, e.g., Pinches 1998 and Borison 2003). One can still attempt to value the claim W using a replicating portfolio (spanning). Though, because the markets are incomplete no single replicating portfolio exactly mirrors the value of the claim. Such valuation models can be labelled partial spanning models (see, e.g., Henderson 2005). Merton (1998) recognizes the need for partial spanning models in incomplete markets and gives an example of a replicating portfolio (see equation (4.23)), which duplicates the option payoffs as much as possible using traded market assets.

(4.23) $$W_N = \bar{a}_0 B_t + \bar{a}_1 X_1 + \bar{a}_2 X_2 + \ldots + \bar{a}_n X_n \quad \text{, with } \bar{a}_i \text{ for } i = 0,1,\ldots,n$$

where

W_N = duplicating portfolio
$\bar{a}_i$ = portfolio weights

W_N is the projection onto the subspace of marketed pure-state claims X and the risk-free bond B_t in order to duplicate the random payoff from the new claim W, which is to be priced by solving for all the $\bar{a}_i$. Because the market is incomplete, an error term e (in terms of minimum expected squared error of the duplicating portfolio; see, e.g., Luenberger 2001 and Luenberger 2002, p. 1114) shows up as a result of the difference between the payoffs of the replicating portfolio W_N and the payoffs of the claim W. The optimal solution of equation (4.23) is given by the $\bar{a}_i$, which minimize e in equation (4.24).

(4.24) $$e = E\left[(W - W_N)^2\right]$$

Kogut and Kulatilaka (2001, p. 752) refer to this error term e as a "tracking error" and state that: "This error is akin to basis risk in commodity markets where the price of a commodity is specific to its location". Thus the question about a potential violation of the no-arbitrage condition to asset valuation is raised. Kogut and Kulatilaka (2001) affirm that risk-neutral valuation is viable as long as the error components are independent and have no systematic risk.[44] Based only on market data and no further assumptions regarding investor risk preferences, the claim can be priced within lower and upper boundaries using the approach in equation (4.23) and equation (4.24) (refer to Ng and Bjornsson 2001 and Luenberger 2002 for examples of this approach in valuing real options). As is the case with complete markets any value of the claim outside the identified interval immediately introduces an opportunity for arbitrage (riskless profit). As the market becomes increasingly complete the bounds collapse (see, e.g., Smith and Nau 1995, p. 805, for an example of this in valuing a production plant).

If one wishes to narrow the interval, additional assumptions are required. Depending on the lack of market completeness the Fisher (1930) separation theorem partially breaks down. As mentioned above the theorem applies to complete markets, and in incomplete markets the separation of the investment and financing decisions of corporation ownership is no longer fully given (see, e.g., Smith and Nau 1995, p. 806, and Smith and McCardle 1998, p. 200). Smith and Nau (1995), Smith and McCardle (1998), and Henderson (2005) develop an "integrated" valuation procedure for partially complete

[44] In terms of the CAPM the components have $\mathrm{cov}(R_M, R_e) = 0$

markets. In particular they make an assumption regarding the risk preferences of company ownership (the second derivative of total utility is negative). Valuing claims in this manner is a non-trivial task.

Utilizing an integrated valuation procedure for partially complete markets consists of two basic phases. First, project cash flow uncertainties are explicitly identified either as market or private risks. Second, the project cash flows are valued according the underlying uncertainties. If project cash flows are determined (spanned) by market risks, they are valued using the standard risk-neutral probability measure and the risk-free rate. This is the approach described in equation (4.19). If project cash flows are not determined (spanned) by market risks, these cash flows are influenced by private uncertainties. There are two feasible valuation approaches in order to account for private risks. Both use subjective management estimates (e.g., expert estimates) about future cash flows but account for risk in two different ways.

1) The first alternative is to use subjective probabilities about future cash flows and discount these at the risk-free rate. This first approach presumes diversified company owners, who are risk-neutral towards private risks because of their diversification in other assets (see, e.g., McDonald and Siegel 1986). This is similar to the CAPM assumption regarding asset valuation where private (unsystematic) risks do not contribute to an asset's equilibrium return.

2) The second approach to valuing private risks presumes risk-aversion to private risks. Consequently, a risk-averse utility function is applied. Cash flows are again forecasted using subjective probabilities and then discounted at the risk-free rate to find the PV. Subsequently these PVs are inserted into the utility function in order to generate effective certainty equivalents (ECE) (see, e.g., Smith and McCardle 1998). The certainty equivalents represent the compensation the decision-maker would require to give up the right to the project.

Both approaches can be shown to give identical results in the limit. When the correlation coefficient between the replicating portfolio (equation (4.23)) W_N and the project W approaches 1 the error term (see equation (4.24)) approaches 0 (Henderson 2005). In practice the end-result is a valuation interval depending on the degree of correlation (or equivalently the degree of market completeness).

The valuation complexity is reduced by making the assumption that there exists a 'single agent', who optimizes the expected utility for consumption (Smith and McCardle 1998, pp. 199-200). Likewise Henderson (2005) discusses the advantage of using the assumption of a single owner-manager in the valuation. Still, the use of a utility function is problematic because it does not take into account other investment opportunities in the market. Therefore, the use of a utility function is sensible only when valuing the private (or unsystematic risks) inherent in the payoff vector from the claim (see, e.g., De Reyck, Degraeve, and Gustafsson 2004 for a discussion of this point). Further, the resulting project value is difficult to interpret in terms of shareholder value because of the employed underlying restrictions regarding the preference function. Multiple owners with differing utility functions and consumption preferences would need an extension of the basic valuation model.

It is sensible to recapitulate the above discussion of asset valuation in general when markets are either complete or incomplete. The following two-by-two matrix illustrates the valuation choices as they shall be considered for this thesis (see Table 8).

Table 8: Asset Valuation - Market Completeness and Risk Preferences

Markets are... / *Risk Preference Assumption*	*complete*	*incomplete*
Risk-Aversion	Equilibrium Pricing Model	Integrated Valuation Model: • market risks: risk-neutral • private risks: risk-averse
Risk-Neutrality	Martingale Pricing Model	Integrated Valuation Model: • market risks: risk-neutral • private risks: risk-neutral

Source: Own creation

Regarding the automobile development process the actual degree of completeness depends on the specific project at hand. There is an inherent problem concerning the degree of market completeness when valuing corporate resources and capabilities. Per definition a capability is unique to the organization and cannot easily be duplicated. Therefore, applying financial economics to the valuation of unique characteristics of the organization leads to the challenge of finding assets, which yield information about the resulting payoff profiles. If it were possible to perfectly span the payoffs resulting from a capability using other marketed assets, the capability cannot be unique, since it could be easily duplicated. The problem, which arises due to the unique capability, is therefore a difficulty of finding marketed assets, which function as inputs in a real option valuation using a risk-neutral method.

Therefore, in the case of the automotive development process, markets must generally be assumed incomplete, due to the existence of unique resources and capabilities. This is also a common trait of development process valuation models (Copeland and Antikarov 2001). Because of the lack of market completeness the above-mentioned market-discipline partially ceases to exist because the markets no longer price the additional sources of risk in the project, and risk-neutral valuation cannot be solely applied. This is what Amram and Kulatilaka (1999, p. 98) refer to as a "decision's distance from the market." Consequently, for this work an integrated valuation model (see Table 8) of the development process will be applied.

4.3 Option Valuation

Until now, the models for asset valuation in general have been outlined and their assumptions discussed. The following sections shall focus on presenting a valuation model for the automotive development process, with a particular focus on the inherent real options.

4.3.1 Valuing Financial and Real Options[45]

Due to the similar structure between financial and real options (see Appendix 2), the valuation models for financial options can be applied equally to real options. There are basically two methods available for valuing options: analytical and numerical techniques (see Figure 30).

Figure 30: Option Pricing Techniques

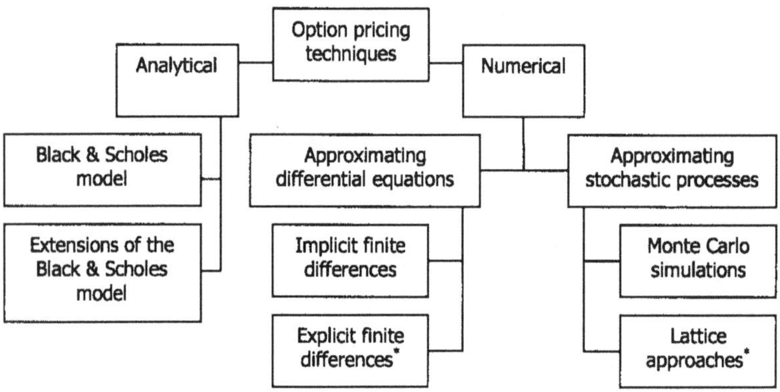

* In some cases these overlap.

Source: own creation, refer in general to Geske and Shastri (1985) and Hull (2003)

In general, simpler options can be valued using analytical techniques. This is particularly true for options with one underlying and of the European type. A well-known example of this approach is the seminal paper by Black and Scholes (1973) for the valuation of a European call option. Applied to the valuation of real options the analytical techniques were the basis for some of the first academic contributions (refer in general to Dixit and Pindyck 1994 and Trigeorgis 2000 for an overview of some of the most important analytical models). The analytic approaches often employ some form of Bellman's

[45] For a general introduction to the subject of real options please refer to Trigeorgis (2000).

Principle of Optimality (Dixit and Pindyck 1994, p. 100), which is basically a dynamic programming approach. Though, in the case of American options and options with several underlyings the analytic approaches become difficult or even impossible to solve (see, e.g., the argumentation of Childs et al. 1999 for valuing contingent claims in a development process using a numerical method).

In practice the numerical techniques are frequently applied to value options. The reasons are twofold. First, numerical techniques can be utilized to value most options. Second, numerical techniques are much easier to apprehend and communicate. Hence, numerical techniques shall be used primarily for this thesis. Within the numerical techniques, the first group focuses on "approximating the partial differential equation with a system of difference equations" (Kamrad and Ritchken 1991, p. 1640), which can then be solved (subject to an assumption regarding the stochastic price process followed by the underlying and certain boundary conditions) to attain the option value. The second group of approaches concentrates either on approximating the stochastic price process followed by the underlying or using simulation techniques to model the price process followed by the underlying. The simulation techniques have the advantage of being fairly straightforward to implement. The downside lies in the fact that not all option types can be valued using simulation approaches, and the simulation model in practice quickly becomes a "black box" (see, e.g., Trigeorgis 2000, p. 55). The second group of methods approximating the stochastic process are the lattice approaches. A very well-known approach is the paper by Cox, Ross, and Rubenstein (1979), which solves for the value of a European Option using a binomial process (lattice approach, see Figure 30) to approximate the process (geometric Brownian motion) followed by the underlying. The Black and Scholes (1973) result can be found to be a special case of the binomial model by Cox, Ross, and Rubenstein (1979) in the limit. In the case of real options, the lattice approaches are widely employed by academics and practitioners alike, and particularly the binomial process is put to use (refer in general to Trigeorgis

2000 and Copeland and Antikarov 2001).[46] The lattice approaches shall therefore by employed primarily to value the automotive development process.

4.3.2 Real Options in the Automobile Development Process

On several occasions this thesis has concentrated on identifying managerial flexibility, uncertainty, and irreversibility in both the point- and set-based models of automotive development. These factors are important, because they indicate the existence of real options. Chapter 3 defined and argued for the role of capabilities in the automotive development process. A particular emphasis was placed on the development model at Toyota and their specific capabilities. Chapter 4 has until now linked capabilities with real options. Consequently, it is now in line to discuss the automotive development process from the real options' lens in order to find the most valuable development process setup (see also equation (4.1)).

The challenge at this point is to pinpoint the real option(s), which shall be analyzed in more detail. Since there are many managerial flexibilities and uncertainties during the development process, there are consequently an infinite number of real options to be analyzed. The 'true' value (in terms of ENPV, see, e.g., equation (4.1)) of the automotive development process would represent all the identified real options. This is a nearly impossible task. Still, it is possible to approximate the value of all the real options. Trigeorgis (2000, pp. 232-240) discusses the effect of real option interactions, which can take place when more than option are based on the same underlying. These interactions depend on the option types (call or put), the degree of separation of their exercise times, their relative degree of being in or out of the money, and their sequential order. All these factors effect the probability of joint exercise and thereby the value of the options.

In the following, an approximation to the true value of the automotive development process is made by identifying a few 'dominant' real options as stand-ins for the value of a given automotive development process setup. Once again, the development process

---

[46] Refer also to Appendix 3 for an illustration of the real option valuation process in practice

at Toyota is of particular interest and shall serve as a starting case so as to detect the important real option(s). Figure 29 lists Toyota's component and architectural capabilities as identified in chapter 3. Figure 31 extends the figure and adds the viewpoint of the financial markets to Toyota's development process.

Figure 31: Toyota's Capabilities from the Real Options View

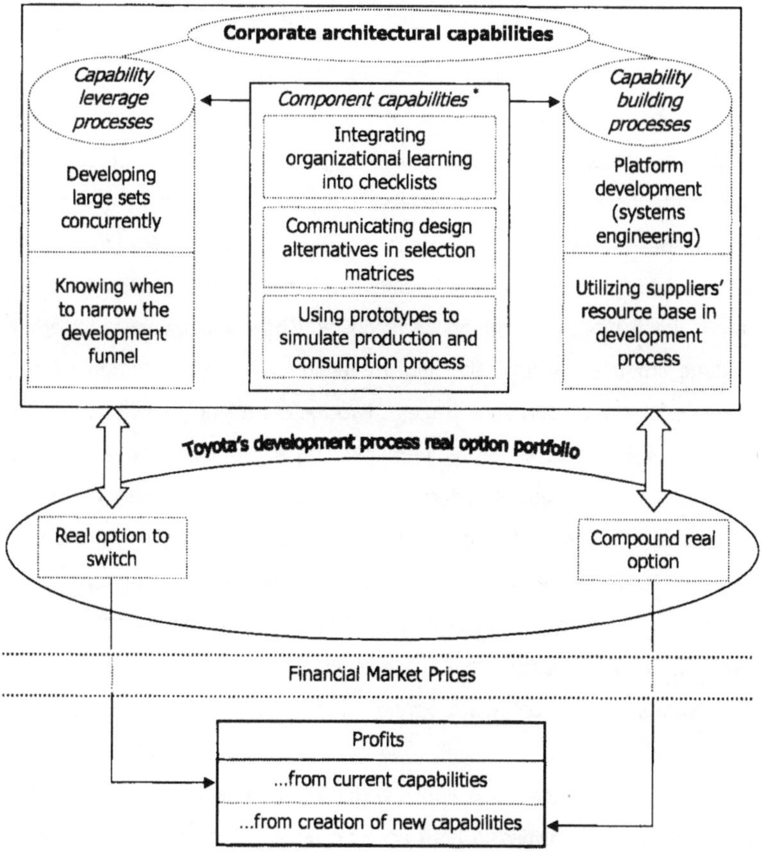

* *Note:* Toyota's assets are not depicted

Source: own creation

The bottom half of Figure 31 mirrors the listed capabilities in the form of a 'real option to switch' and a 'compound real option' respectively. In order to use the discipline of the markets, the objective is to value these two options using primarily financial market prices (for market risks) and expert estimates (for private risks) (see also the lower right quadrant in Table 8).

Carr (1993) shows that the exchange option, which gives the owner the right to exchange one asset for another, can be viewed as a general form of many types of options, e.g, call and put options. This is also the case for the identified options. In Figure 31 the compound real option (Geske 1979), based on the architectural capabilities, is most likely the most valuable of the two options as it applies to all corporate projects on a global scale, not only to a single automotive project. It is very much concerned with innovation and sustainable competitive advantage due to the architectural capabilities in platforms and supplier cooperations. Both take place in the most uncertain and valuable circumstances. In addition, the architectural capabilities are dynamic in nature, implying large amounts of flexibility. The combination of uncertain environments, large amounts of flexibility, and irreversibility make the compound real option very valuable for the corporation. Though, two factors make the compound real option irrelevant for this work, which is primarily concerned with the automotive development process (see the problem statement). First, it is likely to be very difficult to identify the correct parameters for this option because it is derived from two dynamic capabilities, which in turn (per definition) are difficult to classify on an operative level. Second, the compound option applies to all corporate projects due to the architechtural capabilities involved. For this reason it is difficult to establish a conversion key, which could attribute portions of the compound option value to an individual development project.

The real option to switch is the second and final option identified in Figure 31. It is based mainly on Toyota's capabilities in both opening up and subsequently narrowing the development funnel. I.e., the option to switch can be related directly to a single automotive development project. At the same time, large parts of this thesis argued for the uniqueness and importance of Toyota's set-based development capabilities. It is therefore very appealing to value the option to switch as the dominant option in Toyota's development process.

4.3.3 The Real Option to Switch in the Automobile Development Process

Figure 15 showed the concept of modularity as applied to the automotive set-based development process. In the example four design alternatives are developed in parallel. Analyzed as a European option, the option to switch allows management to choose the most valuable of the design alternatives for implementation at the expiration date, e.g., 1 year before mass production. Therefore, the switch option modelled here is a call. Understood as an American option to switch, at any point in time management has the flexibility to switch resources during the course of the automotive development process to the most promising design alternative(s). In both the case of the European and American options the resource investments are irreversible to some degree and depend on the unfolding market and technical uncertainties for each design alternative respectively.

Table 4 compared the point- and set-based strategies in terms of several variables, which can also be encompassed as part of a real options model. The information contained in Table 4 was further developed and illustrated graphically in Figure 18, which, based on the analyses of the point- and set-based models of automotive development in practice, illustrates how there is a trade-off between the value of the flexibility to switch and the incremental investment costs of doing so. The value of the flexibility to switch in Figure 18 is modelled here in the form of an option to switch. The uncertainties driving the value of the option to switch are the market and technical risks for each design alternative respectively. Consequently, the value of the flexibility to switch formally depends *n* underlyings and two risk sources per underlying. Using this approach, the point-based development process is a special case of the more general set-based development process, namely when the set size equals 1. This is illustrated in Figure 32.

Figure 32: The Option to Switch in the Automobile Development Process

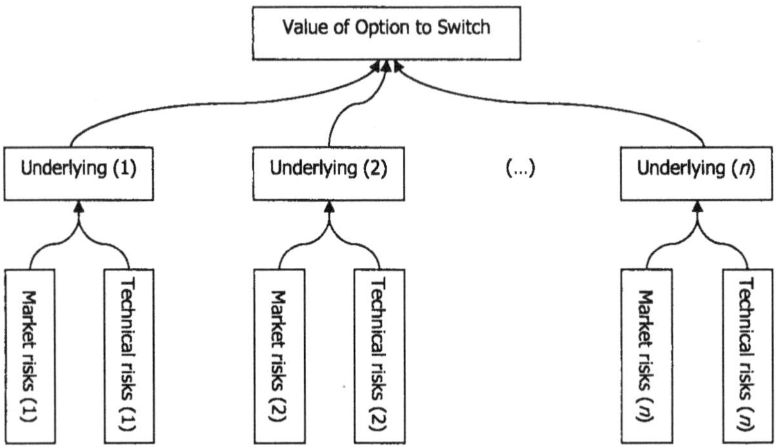

Source: own creation

The value of the option to switch is a multivariate contingent claim (or equivalently a 'rainbow option') with two underlying sources of uncertainty (technical and market) for each underlying. This is a complex option to model. Until recently not many attempts have been made in the real options literature valuing options with more than one underlying. Regarding the development process Childs, Ott, and Triantis (1998) develop a continuous-time state-space model of a generic development process. Their model allows for the handling of two separate design alternatives (two underlyings), which follow a bivariate normal distribution with correlation coefficient ρ. The model cannot value an option on more than two underlyings. In a setup similar to this work, they classify various development strategies ranging from a sequential (point-based) to a parallel (set-based) strategy. The value of the option to switch can be determined as the difference between the value of a sequential setup and a parallel setup.[47]

Childs and Triantis (1999) develop a discrete-time state-space model of a generic development process. Their model also allows for the modelling of two design alternatives, which can be developed following a sequential or parallel development process. This model can also not value an option on more than two underlyings. Childs and Triantis (1999) assume that the value of each of the design alternatives (S_i, $i = a,b$) follows geometric Brownian motion $dS_i = \mu_i S_i dt + \sigma_i S_i \varepsilon_i \sqrt{dt}$ where ε_i is a normally distributed variable with mean of 0 and a standard deviation of 1. Further, S_a and S_b are correlated with correlation coefficient ρ. In order to value the development project, first, each of the variables is approximated by a trinomial lattice where the first and second moments of the continuous-time process are matched with the discrete approximation. Second, because S_a and S_b are both trinomially distributed a two-dimensional lattice is constructed from the two individual lattices with 9 (= 3 x 3) nodes emanating from each point in time-state space. Accordingly, there are 9 probabilities, one for each node. Each probability incorporates the correlation coefficient between S_a and S_b as well as the respective volatilities. Finally, the project values (including option values) are calculated contingent on the values of the two underlying assets in the combined lattice and the t_0-value of the development project is found using the standard recursive dynamic programming algorithm (see, e.g., Cox, Ross, and Rubenstein 1979).

4.4 The Option to Switch as a Multivariate Contingent Claim

The following model is closely related to the models of Childs, Ott, and Triantis (1998) and Childs and Triantis (1999). It also sets out to value the option to switch with more

[47] Refer also to Sorensen (2001) for an analysis and a computer program of the model from Childs, Ott, and Triantis (1998).

than one underlying. The model makeup can be considered an extension of Boyle's (1988) model, which extended the Cox, Ross, and Rubenstein (1979) binomial method in order to handle two underlyings for the valuation of a contingent claim. The approach taken here is also close in spirit to the original Cox, Ross, and Rubenstein (1979) method. Though, it is more general and allows for *n* underlyings.

4.4.1 Model Assumptions

Based on the previous chapters it is essential to list some general assumptions for the valuation of the automobile development process for the time period in question.[48] The below assumptions all have a twofold purpose. First of all, they are necessary in order for the structure of valuation model to be correct. Second of all, they act as minimum requirements, thereby allowing the focus of the thesis to be on the structure of the valuation model.

1) First, markets are presumed incomplete. I.e., risk-neutral valuation is possible only partly and under the assumption that company ownership is risk-neutral towards private risks. The further the distance of a business process from the financial markets, the more difficult it is to span FCFs with marketed assets. The assumption about risk-neutrality towards private risks is a convenient assumption to make because it puts aside the need for a specification of risk-adverse preference functions, which is a non-trivial task, particularly when there are several owners with varying risk-preferences. In addition, the assumption about risk-neutrality towards private risks is widespread in the real-option literature and often employed.

2) Second, for the purpose of this work, financial markets are assumed perfect. The implications of e.g., taxes and financial market structure are disregarded. The model could be extended to coincide with these imperfections. Still, this assumption prevents the valuation model from becoming unnecessarily complicated and most likely has a minor effect on the issue of optimal development process structure on an overall level.

---

[48] Refer also to the assumptions made by Black and Scholes (1973, pp. 640-641) in their seminal work on option pricing.

3) Third, financial markets are assumed arbitrage-free. This is a necessary precondition for the martingale measure to be applied.

4) Fourth, the stochastic properties of both the stochastic variables and processes in question are presumed stationary.

5) Fifth, the risk-free rate (r), the volatility of asset returns (σ_i), and the correlation (ρ_{ij}) between assets i and j are assumed constant.

4.4.2 Boyle, Evnine, and Gibbs (1989) – An n-Dimensional Lattice

Contingent claims whose values depend on several sources of uncertainty are often observed in the financial industry. It will be shown that the automobile development process also contains such a claim. Unfortunately analytical solutions for such claims are rare, thereby prompting the use of numerical techniques. The option to switch is purposeful for the modelling purposes as management has the flexibility to choose between the different underlyings available, and no underlying has yet been chosen (see also Figure 32). Boyle, Evnine, and Gibbs (1989) (BEG) present a model, which allows for the numerical modelling and subsequent valuation of the option to switch when there are n underlying assets. Regarding this work, each design alternative or prototype represents one underlying asset in the model. Kamrad and Ritchken (1991) also develop a numerical valuation technique for multivariate claims, which is similar to the BEG approach. Their model is also based on approximating the logarithmic returns process by a discrete multinomial lattice. Their model though generalizes the results of the BEG approach and in addition allows for horizontal jumps. Choosing not to explicitly model jumps in the underlying stochastic price processes, the BEG model shall be applied in the following because it has the potential for offering new insights into the valuation and optimal structure of the automobile development process. Especially the previously mentioned trade-off between investment costs and the increased value of flexibility is of interest.

As with the standard binomial tree (Cox, Ross, and Rubenstein 1979), the BEG model basically consists of two components: the jump amplitudes and the jump probabilities. These components must be chosen so that the mean and standard deviation of the discrete distribution converges to the mean and standard deviation of the continuous distribution. The lattice structure also allows for the analysis of European and American type options. In developing the BEG model there are two development choices. The first option is to fix the jump probabilities and then solve for the jump amplitudes. The second development option is to fix the jump amplitudes and then determine the jump probabilities to ensure convergence. This second variant is the approach taken by Cox, Ross, and Rubenstein (1979), and BEG also develop their model in this manner.

According with the arguments specified in relation to Table 8 the integrated approach is chosen for this work. Therefore, the underlying asset, S_i, is specifed as the present value of te expected cash flows resulting from the development process assuming no management flexibility to deviate from the original plan. To begin with, it is assumed that each underlying asset follows geometric Brownian motion

(4.25) $$dS_i = \mu_i S_i dt + \sigma_i S_i dz_i \qquad 1 \le i \le n$$

where

S_i = the current price of asset i

μ_i = the drift of the process for asset i

dz_i = a Gauss-Wiener process

ρ_{ij} = the instantaneous correlation between dz_i and dz_j, $1 \le i \le j \le n$

In the case of the automotive development process S_i stands for the stochastic progress of the value of design alternative i. The next step is to specify the differential equation, which must be satisfied by the value of the derivative. For the case of one underlying asset (stock) Black, Scholes, and Merton (BSM) employ the stochastic differential equation (see, e.g., Merton 1973, p. 164),

(4.26) $$\frac{\partial f}{\partial t} + rS_i \frac{\partial f}{\partial S_i} + \frac{1}{2}\sigma_i^2 S_i^2 \frac{\partial^2 f}{\partial S_i^2} = rf$$

where

f = value of derivative

which must be satisfied by the value of the derivative. Garman (1976) and Cox, Ingersoll, and Ross (1985) extend the BSM differential equation and develop a stochastic differential equation (see equation (4.27)) for a derivative with a payoff depending on n underlying assets.

(4.27)
$$rf = \frac{\partial f}{\partial t} + \sum_{i=1}^{n} S_i \frac{\partial f}{\partial S_i}(\mu_i - \lambda_i\sigma_i) + \frac{1}{2}\sum_{i=1}^{n}\sum_{j=1}^{n} \rho_{ij}\sigma_i\sigma_j S_i S_j \frac{\partial^2 f}{\partial S_i \partial S_j}$$

As with the BSM stochastic differential equation the specific knowledge of the investor's risk preferences (embodied in μ_i; see equation (4.20)) becomes irrelevant, because λ_i is known. This is the previously stated link between CCA and DP (see equation (4.22)). In the case of the value of the automotive development process, f is the value of the option to switch between the n design alternative(s) being developed concurrently. Equivalently, in the case of Toyota's automotive development process, f in the following stands for the value of the capability leverage processes (Figure 29), which make possible the option to choose the maximum value of the n available design alternatives. I.e., this is the set-based approach to the development process.

Because an asset following geometric Brownian motion is lognormally distributed at any point in time the n assets together have a multivariate lognormal distribution. Instead of solving the differential equation in equation (4.27) directly with the appropriate boundary conditions, BEG make use of the before mentioned approach used by Cox, Ross, and Rubenstein (1979) and approximate discretely the stochastic processes taken by the n underlying assets in equation (4.25). The goal is to have the discrete distribution converge to the multivariate lognormal distribution in the limit. In order to do this, the discrete approximation must match the corresponding moments in the continuous-time state-space stochastic process.

The following additional notation is introduced in accordance with the approach taken by BEG:

T = time to option maturity in years
X = exercise price of option
N = number of time steps into which the time T is divided
h = T/N; length of a time step
$S_i u_i$ = asset value after one up-jump
$S_i d_i$ = asset value after one down-jump
μ_i = $r - 1/2\,\sigma_i^2$ = drift-rate of continuous lognormal distribution

BEG present the appropriate jump probabilities and jump sizes for the case when n=2 but give only the general formula for the n-asset case. The up and down jump sizes (u_i and d_i respectively) are chosen to conform to the Cox, Ross, and Rubenstein (1979) notation (shown in equation (4.11)). For the n-asset case the formulas are in general

(4.28) $$u_i d_i = 1 \qquad i = 1, 2, \ldots, n$$

where

(4.29) $$u_i = e^{\sigma_i \sqrt{h}} \qquad i = 1, 2, \ldots, n$$

Because the stochastic processes are stationary the u_i and d_i are 'fixed' for the time period T. For the case when n=2 there are four ($= 2 \times 2$) possible states after one time step corresponding to the number of possible combinations of two assets. Equivalently, there are four jump probabilities, one for each state. Analogous to previous notation used e.g. in connection with the binomial tree (chapter 4.2.4) the probabilities are labelled q in order to emphasize that they are probabilities under a martingale measure. This is seen in Table 9.

Table 9: The State-Space with 2 Assets

Nature of Jumps	*Probability*	*Asset Pair Prices*
Up, up	$q_1 = q_{uu}$	S_1u_1, S_2u_2
Up, down	$q_2 = q_{ud}$	S_1u_1, S_2d_2
Down, up	$q_3 = q_{du}$	S_1d_1, S_2u_2
Down, down	$q_4 = q_{dd}$	S_1d_1, S_2d_2

Source: Boyle, Evnine, and Gibbs (1989, p. 245); own creation

Together, the jump sizes in equation (4.29) and the probabilities in Table 9 approximate the bivariate lognormal density in the limit. For the case when *n*=2 BEG in detail show how to find the four probabilities given in Table 9.[49] These are seen in Equations (4.30) - (4.33).

(4.30) $$q_1 = \frac{1}{4}\left(1 + \rho + \sqrt{h}\left(\frac{\mu_1}{\sigma_1} + \frac{\mu_2}{\sigma_2}\right)\right)$$

(4.31) $$q_2 = \frac{1}{4}\left(1 - \rho + \sqrt{h}\left(\frac{\mu_1}{\sigma_1} - \frac{\mu_2}{\sigma_2}\right)\right)$$

(4.32) $$q_3 = \frac{1}{4}\left(1 - \rho + \sqrt{h}\left(-\frac{\mu_1}{\sigma_1} + \frac{\mu_2}{\sigma_2}\right)\right)$$

(4.33) $$q_4 = \frac{1}{4}\left(1 + \rho + \sqrt{h}\left(-\frac{\mu_1}{\sigma_1} - \frac{\mu_2}{\sigma_2}\right)\right)$$

Because the $q_j\ (j = 1, 2, \ldots, 4)$ are probabilities the final restriction is that they all sum to one.

(4.34) $$q_1 + q_2 + q_3 + q_4 = 1$$

---

[49] Refer to Boyle, Evnine, and Gibbs (1989, pp. 245-246).

The formulas for the discrete approximation of the *n*-dimensional multivariate lognormal distribution are presented in the following. As in the case when *n*=2 each asset can take either an up- or down-jump after one time step *h*. The jump sizes remain defined as in equations (4.28) and (4.29). Analogous to equation (4.34) the probabilities in *n*-asset case must sum to one.

(4.35) $$\sum_{j=1}^{M} q_j = 1$$

where

$M = 2^n =$ the number of states after one time period h

For the calculation of the *M* risk-neutral probabilities BEG specify equation (4.36).

(4.36) $$q_j = \frac{1}{M}\left(1 + \sum_{\substack{k,m=1\\k<m}}^{n} \delta_{km}(j)\rho_{km} + \sqrt{h}\sum_{k=1}^{n}\delta_k(j)\frac{\mu_k}{\sigma_k}\right) \qquad j = 1, 2, \ldots, M$$

where

$$\delta_{km}(j) = \begin{cases} 1 \text{ if both asset } k \text{ and asset } m \text{ have jumps in the same direction} \\ \text{in state } j \\ -1 \text{ if both asset } k \text{ and asset } m \text{ have jumps in opposite directions} \\ \text{in state } j \end{cases}$$

$$\delta_k(j) = \begin{cases} 1 \text{ if asset } k \text{ has an up-jump in state } j \\ -1 \text{ if asset } k \text{ has a down-jump in state } j \end{cases}$$

Equations (4.36) and (4.29) together provide the required parameters for constructing a lattice of asset price movements and subsequently computing the value of the derivate asset *f* applying a recursive dynamic programming algorithm.

Of particular interest are the cases when *n*>2. BEG only provide the general formulas in equations (4.36) and (4.29) for these cases. From equation (4.35) it can be seen that the number of probabilities to be calculated grow exponentially with the number of underlying assets.

Table 10: Computational Effort in the BEG Model

Number of Underlyings	*Number of Probabilities*	*Number of States after 2 time steps*
1	2	3
2	4	9
3	8	27

Source: own creation

The Cox, Ross, and Rubenstein (1979) model is represented by the first row in Table 10, when n=1. Table 10 also shows how the number of states after two time steps increases tremendously as the number of underlyings increase. Due to computational limitations for this thesis and illustrative purposes, the case when n=3 shall be considered as a final example. The general formula for the eight probabilities to be calculated is given by equation (4.36), and the particular probabilities presented below.

(4.37)

$$q_1 = \frac{1}{8}\begin{pmatrix} 1+\delta_{12}(1)\rho_{12}+\delta_{13}(1)\rho_{13}+\delta_{23}(1)\rho_{23}+ \\ \sqrt{h}\left[\delta_1(1)\frac{\mu_1}{\sigma_1}+\delta_2(1)\frac{\mu_2}{\sigma_2}+\delta_3(1)\frac{\mu_3}{\sigma_3}\right] \end{pmatrix} \Leftrightarrow$$

$$q_1 = \frac{1}{8}\left(1+\rho_{12}+\rho_{13}+\rho_{23}+\sqrt{h}\left[\frac{\mu_1}{\sigma_1}+\frac{\mu_2}{\sigma_2}+\frac{\mu_3}{\sigma_3}\right]\right)$$

(4.38)

$$q_2 = \frac{1}{8}\begin{pmatrix} 1+\delta_{13}(2)\rho_{13}+\delta_{12}(2)\rho_{12}+\delta_{23}(2)\rho_{23}+ \\ \sqrt{h}\left[\delta_1(2)\frac{\mu_1}{\sigma_1}+\delta_2(2)\frac{\mu_2}{\sigma_2}+\delta_3(2)\frac{\mu_3}{\sigma_3}\right] \end{pmatrix} \Leftrightarrow$$

$$q_2 = \frac{1}{8}\left(1+\rho_{12}-\rho_{13}-\rho_{23}+\sqrt{h}\left[\frac{\mu_1}{\sigma_1}+\frac{\mu_2}{\sigma_2}-\frac{\mu_3}{\sigma_3}\right]\right)$$

(4.39)

$$q_3 = \frac{1}{8}\begin{pmatrix} 1+\delta_{12}(3)\rho_{12}+\delta_{13}(3)\rho_{13}+\delta_{23}(3)\rho_{23}+ \\ \sqrt{h}\left[\delta_1(3)\frac{\mu_1}{\sigma_1}+\delta_2(3)\frac{\mu_2}{\sigma_2}+\delta_3(3)\frac{\mu_3}{\sigma_3}\right] \end{pmatrix} \Leftrightarrow$$

$$q_3 = \frac{1}{8}\left(1-\rho_{12}+\rho_{13}-\rho_{23}+\sqrt{h}\left[\frac{\mu_1}{\sigma_1}-\frac{\mu_2}{\sigma_2}+\frac{\mu_3}{\sigma_3}\right]\right)$$

(4.40)

$$q_4 = \frac{1}{8}\begin{pmatrix} 1+\delta_{12}(4)\rho_{12}+\delta_{13}(4)\rho_{13}+\delta_{23}(4)\rho_{23}+ \\ \sqrt{h}\left[\delta_1(4)\frac{\mu_1}{\sigma_1}+\delta_2(4)\frac{\mu_2}{\sigma_2}+\delta_3(4)\frac{\mu_3}{\sigma_3}\right] \end{pmatrix} \Leftrightarrow$$

$$q_4 = \frac{1}{8}\left(1-\rho_{12}-\rho_{13}+\rho_{23}+\sqrt{h}\left[\frac{\mu_1}{\sigma_1}-\frac{\mu_2}{\sigma_2}+\frac{\mu_3}{\sigma_3}\right]\right)$$

(4.41)

$$q_5 = \frac{1}{8}\begin{pmatrix} 1+\delta_{12}(5)\rho_{12}+\delta_{13}(5)\rho_{13}+\delta_{23}(5)\rho_{23}+ \\ \sqrt{h}\left[\delta_1(5)\frac{\mu_1}{\sigma_1}+\delta_2(5)\frac{\mu_2}{\sigma_2}+\delta_3(5)\frac{\mu_3}{\sigma_3}\right] \end{pmatrix} \Leftrightarrow$$

$$q_5 = \frac{1}{8}\left(1-\rho_{12}-\rho_{13}+\rho_{23}+\sqrt{h}\left[-\frac{\mu_1}{\sigma_1}+\frac{\mu_2}{\sigma_2}+\frac{\mu_3}{\sigma_3}\right]\right)$$

(4.42)

$$q_6 = \frac{1}{8}\begin{pmatrix} 1+\delta_{12}(6)\rho_{12}+\delta_{13}(6)\rho_{13}+\delta_{23}(6)\rho_{23}+ \\ \sqrt{h}\left[\delta_1(6)\frac{\mu_1}{\sigma_1}+\delta_2(6)\frac{\mu_2}{\sigma_2}+\delta_3(6)\frac{\mu_3}{\sigma_3}\right] \end{pmatrix} \Leftrightarrow$$

$$q_6 = \frac{1}{8}\left(1-\rho_{12}+\rho_{13}-\rho_{23}+\sqrt{h}\left[-\frac{\mu_1}{\sigma_1}+\frac{\mu_2}{\sigma_2}-\frac{\mu_3}{\sigma_3}\right]\right)$$

(4.43)

$$q_7 = \frac{1}{8}\begin{pmatrix} 1+\delta_{12}(7)\rho_{12}+\delta_{13}(7)\rho_{13}+\delta_{23}(7)\rho_{23}+ \\ \sqrt{h}\left[\delta_1(7)\frac{\mu_1}{\sigma_1}+\delta_2(7)\frac{\mu_2}{\sigma_2}+\delta_3(7)\frac{\mu_3}{\sigma_3}\right] \end{pmatrix} \Leftrightarrow$$

$$q_7 = \frac{1}{8}\left(1+\rho_{12}-\rho_{13}-\rho_{23}+\sqrt{h}\left[-\frac{\mu_1}{\sigma_1}-\frac{\mu_2}{\sigma_2}+\frac{\mu_3}{\sigma_3}\right]\right)$$

(4.44)

$$q_8 = \frac{1}{8}\begin{pmatrix} 1+\delta_{12}(8)\rho_{12}+\delta_{13}(8)\rho_{13}+\delta_{23}(8)\rho_{23}+ \\ \sqrt{h}\left[\delta_1(8)\frac{\mu_1}{\sigma_1}+\delta_2(8)\frac{\mu_2}{\sigma_2}+\delta_3(8)\frac{\mu_3}{\sigma_3}\right] \end{pmatrix} \Leftrightarrow$$

$$q_8 = \frac{1}{8}\left(1+\rho_{12}+\rho_{13}+\rho_{23}+\sqrt{h}\left[-\frac{\mu_1}{\sigma_1}-\frac{\mu_2}{\sigma_2}-\frac{\mu_3}{\sigma_3}\right]\right)$$

Applying equation (4.35) to the results in equations (4.37) - (4.44) verifies that the probabilities all sum to one. Below, the lattices for n = 1, n = 2, and n = 3 are presented in the case of two time steps.

Figure 33: Lattice for the Case when *n*=1

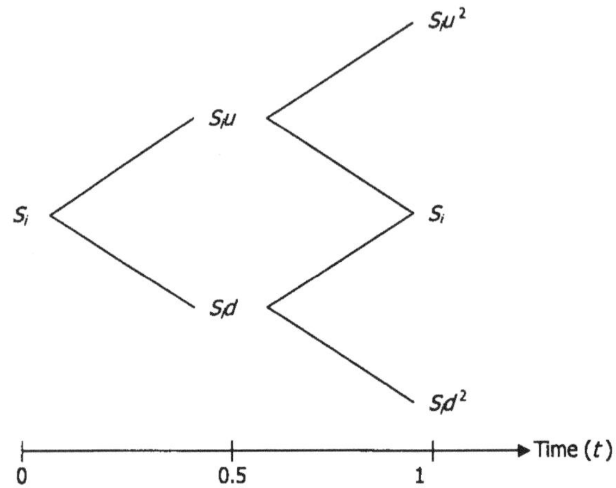

S_i = The starting value of asset i

Source: own creation

Figure 33 shows the lattice for the well-known binomial tree proposed by Cox, Ross, and Rubenstein (1979) in the case of two time steps. The model structure and the movements (lognormal distribution) of the stochastic asset S_i were discussed in chapter 4.2.4. BEG's extension of the binomial tree to the case of two assets, which follow a bivariate lognormal distribution is shown in Figure 34.

Figure 34: Lattice for the Case when *n*=2

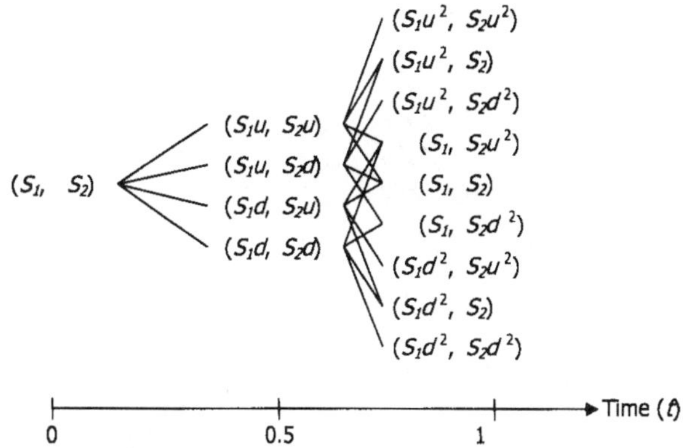

S_i = The starting value of asset i

Source: own creation

The number of nodes now grows according the number of combinations of the two underlying assets. E.g., after one time step (= $t_{0.5}$) there are four (= 2 x 2) combinations of the two underlying assets. The four combinations at $t_{0.5}$ each give rise to four new possible combinations at t_1. Because the tree is recombining there are finally nine nodes at t_1.

Figure 35: Lattice for the Case when *n*=3

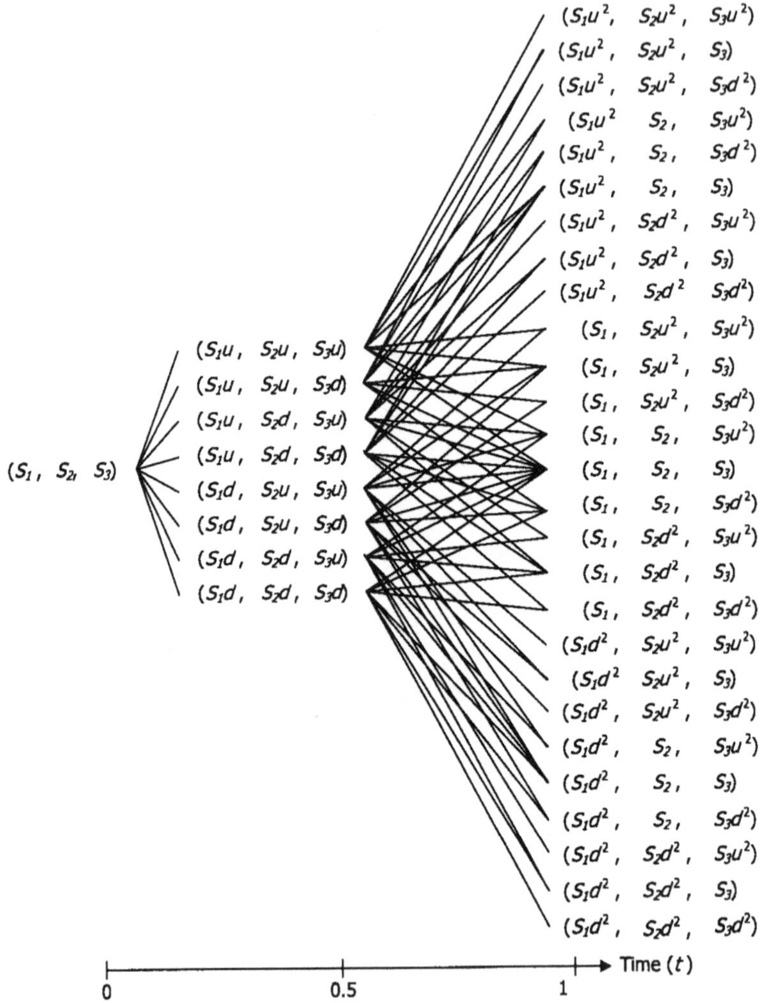

S_i = The starting value of asset i

Source: own creation

Figure 35 shows the lattice for the BEG model in the case of three underlying assets and two time steps. As stated in Table 10 there are now 27 nodes at time t_1.

A special type of switching option is the European option on the maximum of more than one or more assets at t_1. This is the previously identified option in connection with the automobile development process (see also Figure 29). The corresponding intrinsic values of the European option at t_1 are given by

(4.45) $$\max(S_1 - X;\ 0)$$

in the case of n=1,

(4.46) $$\max(S_1 - X;\ S_2 - X;\ 0)$$

in the case of n=2, and finally

(4.47) $$\max(S_1 - X;\ S_2 - X;\ S_3 - X;\ 0)$$

in the case of n=3. In equations (4.45) - (4.47) the variable X represents the discounted present value of the investment outlays required in order to implement a given design alternative. To reiterate, the underlying assets (S_1, S_2, S_3) represent the present values of future expected FCFs resulting from the implementation of a given design alternative. This approach was outlined in the lower right-hand quadrant in Table 8. Copeland and Antikarov (2001, pp.94-95) employ a similar approach, which they call the Marketed Asset Disclaimer (MAD). Once the intrinsic values at each node at t_1 have been calculated, the option value at t_0 is found applying the equivalent martingale measure and the risk-free interest rate.

In order to find the option value of the point-based development processes the lattice in Figure 33 is applied. In point-based development there is only a single design alternative being developed. The evolution of the value of this design alternative with time corresponds to the stochastic price process for S_1 in the lattice. In order to find the value of set-based development one must first identify the number of design alternatives to be developed. When there are two design alternatives being developed the lattice in Figure 34 is applied. Here S_1 and S_2 correspond to the values of the first and second design alternative respectively. When there are three design alternatives the lattice in Figure 35 is applied. Here S_1, S_2, and S_3 correspond to the values of design alternatives one, two, and three respectively. In all three cases the lattices of the underlyings are the starting points for the valuation of the respective option values.

Figure 36 shows the cash flow structure relevant for the valuation of the automobile development process in the case of point-based development.

Figure 36: Cash Flow from the Point-Based Development Process

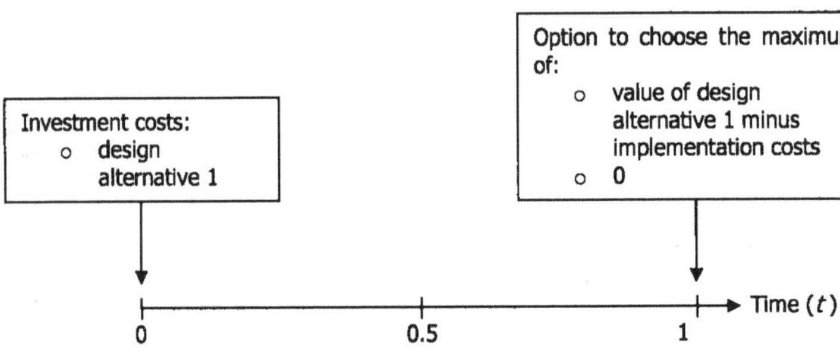

Source: own creation

Figure 37 shows the cash flow structure for the valuation of a set-based development process with two design alternatives.

Figure 37: Cash Flow from the Set-Based Development Process with Two Design Alternatives

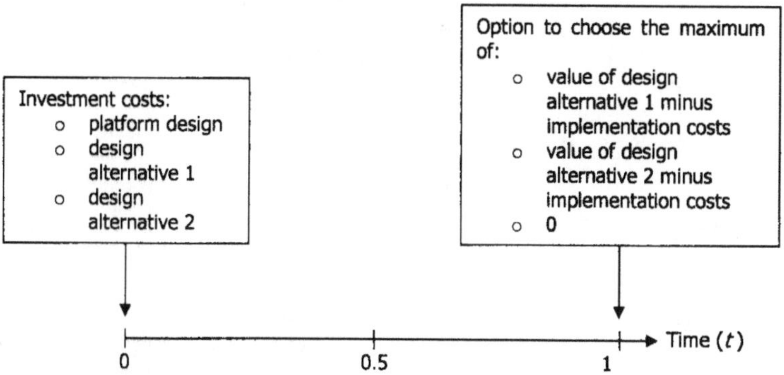

Source: own creation

Figure 37 shows that the set-based development differs from the point-based development process in three respects:

1) First, management now has to pay an upfront investment cost in order to design the automobile platform.

2) Second, the development of more than one design alternative (in this case two designs) has to be financed upfront.

3) Third, in the case of set-based development management now has the choice between more than one design alternative (in this case two designs). This is a direct result of having explored the design space more actively than is the case in point-based development.

Figure 38 shows the cash flows resulting from a set-based development process in the case of three design alternatives being developed concurrently.

Figure 38: Cash Flow from the Set-Based Development Process with Three Design Alternatives

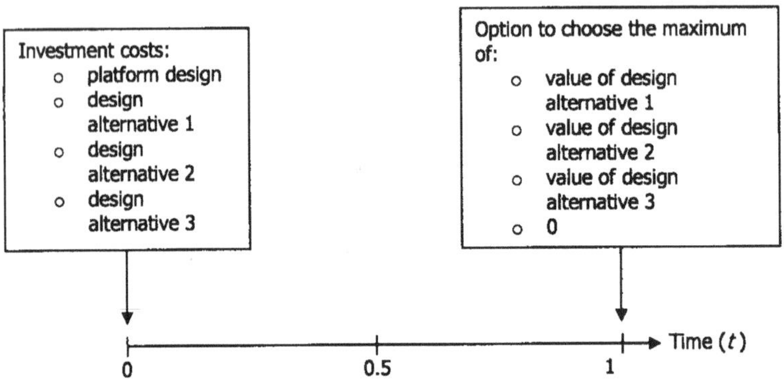

Source: own creation

The value (ENPV) of the automobile development process is then given by

(4.48) $$\text{ENPV} = \text{PV(FCF)} + (\text{Value of Option to Switch}) - (\text{Investment Costs}).$$

Equation (4.48) will be applied extensively in chapter 5 in order to value and optimize the automobile development process. The focus will be on identifying the value drivers for the value of the option to switch. This will allow an in-depth view of optimal resource allocation during the automobile development process.

4.5 Chapter Summary

The first part of this chapter dealt with the role of financial markets in valuing the automotive development process. The so-called discipline of the financial markets states that the prices of marketed securities contain information relevant to the valuation of corporate strategy. It is possible to explain the firm-specific efficiency advantage(s) utilizing a real option valuation model. The utilized approach is to model the corporate decision-making process as resulting in a series of FCFs to be included in a valuation model. Underlying a valuation of the automotive development process is the concept of finding comparable marketed securities, which duplicate the payoffs from the development process. The limitation to this method is given by the open systems nature of strategic management, which makes it difficult to model quantitatively all aspects of the process of sequential choice. Given simplifying arguments it is possible to model the essential causalities in terms of a real option model. Maximizing the value of this model implies finding an optimal automotive development process setup.

The second part of this chapter presented a general valuation framework, with which any claim can be valued. Assuming no-arbitrage and given complete markets it was shown that there exists a unique equivalent martingale measure. The value of a given claim thus equals the expected, discounted value of the claim taken with respect to the martingale measure. Equivalently, if the market price of risk is known, it was shown that the martingale approach (CCA) coincides with the value found using DP. In the case of incomplete markets there exist private risks, which aren't spanned by the prices of marketed securities. This is most likely the case in automotive development when unique capabilities (which per definition cannot be duplicated) give rise to payoff structures. There no longer exists a unique martingale measure, and any duplication of payoffs resulting from the automotive development process now results in a tracking error. In order to value the private risks, an assumption is needed regarding the risk-preference of the owners of the automotive developing company towards the private risks. In this thesis they are presumed risk-neutral towards private risks.

The third part of this chapter briefly gave an overview of option valuation techniques. The focus in this thesis is on identifying the relevant real options for the valuation of the automotive development process. To this purpose the previous analysis of the capabilities in Toyota's automotive development process was taken as a starting point. The option to switch was chosen as the most dominant real option existing within a given automotive development project. This is in concurrence with the observation of development funnels in practice: Widening the mouth of the development funnel ensures a choice between more design alternatives. The value of this option to choose (switch) is driven by the values of the n underlying design alternatives. The strategic problem to solve is therefore how to determine the size (n) of the initial set of design alternatives to be developed.

The fourth part of this chapter presented the BEG model. The option to choose between the n design alternatives is modelled as a multivariate contingent claim. For illustrative purposes, the set size was limited to a maximum of $n = 3$. The equivalent martingale measure was computed in the cases on $n = 2$ and $n = 3$. The resulting lattices were shown in the cases of $n = 1$, $n = 2$, and $n = 3$. Finally, the cash flow structures to be applied in the real option model were shown for $n = 1$, $n = 2$, and $n = 3$.

Chapter 5: Optimizing the Automotive Development Process

The purpose of this chapter is to deal mainly with answering subproblem 4 of the problem statement:
How can management structure the development process in order to maximize its value?

The overall purpose of this chapter is to calculate the optimal size of the set of design alternatives to be developed concurrently. This will be done by primarily utilizing the real option model developed in chapter 4.
This chapter is outlined as follows. The first part analyzes the value of the option to switch with respect to the various value drivers inherent in the BEG model. The objective is present a sensitivity analysis, which can help guide managerial decision making in practice by focusing on the critical value derivers. The second part identifies an optimal development process setup by finding the number of design alternatives, which maximizes the value of the development process. The challenge is to compare the marginal increase in investment costs by increasing the size of the set to be developed concurrently and the marginal positive increase in the value of the option to switch in order to determine the optimal set size. The third part presents and argues for five principles of automotive development, thereby stressing the managerial implications of this work.

5.1 Value Drivers in the Automobile Development Process

Table 11 shows the base case values of the model variables utilized in the following sections.

Table 11: Case Data for the Automobile Development Process

Model Variable	*Base Case Value*	*Description*
T	1	The time length of the development process. In this case the development process takes place during 1 "time unit", i.e., from t_0 to t_1. For reasons of simplicity the total development time is assumed constant in all the calculations.
N	2	During the total development process the underlying variable(s) jump at time t_0 and $t_{0.5}$.
r_f	0.05	The risk-free interest rate. For reasons of simplicity it is assumed constant throughout the development process.
X	100	The exercise price of the European option to switch at t_1. As explained in chapter 4.4.2 it represents the present value of the costs resulting from an implementation of a design alternative. For reasons of simplicity the exercise price is assumed alike for any design alternative. I.e., the base case data assume an at-the-money option
S_i	100	The value of asset i (i = 1, 2, 3) at t_0
σ_i	0.4	The standard deviation of returns of asset i (i = 1, 2, 3). For reasons of simplicity they are assumed constant throughout the development process.
ρ_{ij}	0	The correlation coefficient between assets i and j (i, j = 1, 2, 3). For reasons of simplicity they are assumed constant throughout the development process.

Source: own creation

In the following, the variables S_i, σ_i, and ρ_{ij} are purposefully varied in order to analyze their respective impacts on the option value. All the results are presented in tabular form in Appendix 4. Within the text the results are primarily presented graphically.

5.1.1 The Option Value in the Point-Based Development Process

Figure 36 shows that the option value in the point-based development process arises from the scenarios where the present value of FCFs from implementing the one design alternative is greater than the implementation costs of doing so (see equation (4.45)).

Of interest are therefore the standard deviation and the current value of the design alternative. Both variables positively affect the probability of the option to implement the design alternative being exercised and consequently the current value of the option in the point-based development process. Figure 39 and Figure 40 show the influence of the standard deviation and current value of the design alternative respectively.

Figure 39: The Effect of Volatility with One Design Alternative

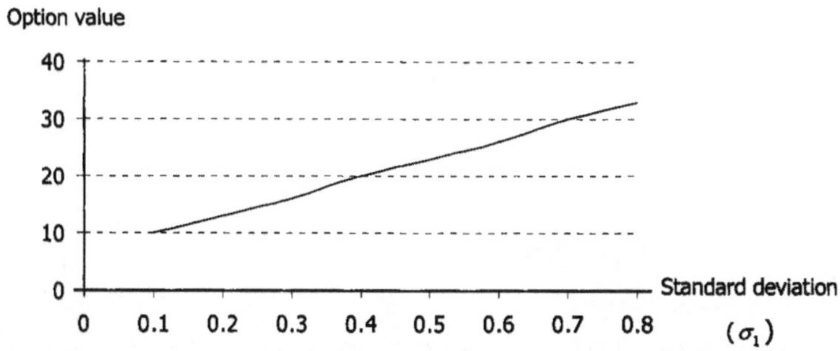

Data: $S_1 = 100$, $X = 100$, $T = 1$, $N = 2$, $r_f = 0.05$

Source: own creation, see also Appendix 4

In the case of point-based development it can be seen that the option value increases linearly with the standard deviation of the design alternative. I.e., for higher risk development projects the option value makes up a sizeable part of the ENPV. The option value in Figure 39 shall serve as a benchmark for the subsequent analyses of the set-based development process. The option values achieved in set-based development will be compared with the point-based case.

Figure 40: The Effect of Underlying Value with One Design Alternative

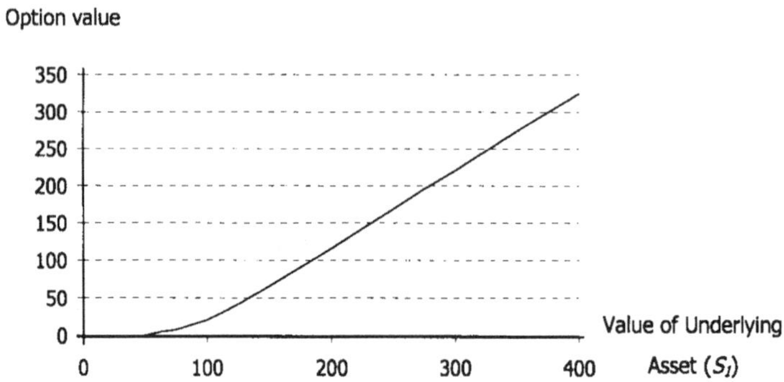

Data: $\sigma_1 = 0.4$, $X = 100$, $T = 1$, $N = 2$, $r_f = 0.05$

Source: own creation, see also Appendix 4

Figure 40 shows that once the current value of the underlying asset is high enough, the option will almost certainly be exercised. This fact makes the option value rise linearly with the value of the underlying asset in the range of $S_1 > 150$.

5.1.2 The Option Value in the Set-Based Development Process

In the case of set-based development there is an additional parameter, which plays a crucial role. This is the correlation coefficient ρ_{ij}.

Figure 41: The Effect of Volatility with Two Design Alternatives

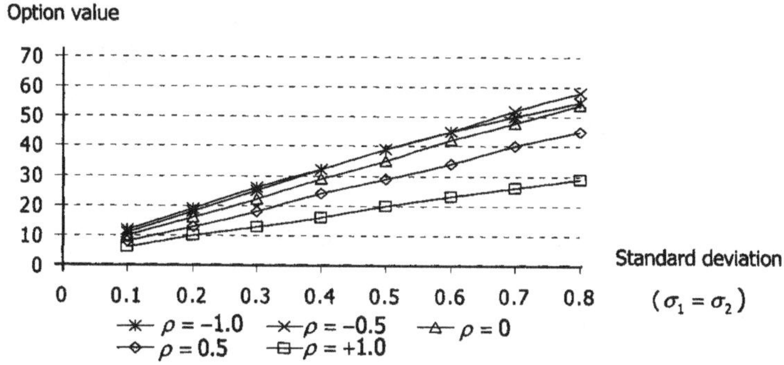

Data: $S_1 = S_2 = 100$, $X = 100$, $T = 1$, $N = 2$, $r_f = 0.05$

Source: own creation, see also Appendix 4

Figure 41 depicts the effect on option value with equal increases in the volatilities of the two underlying assets. Additionally, five different levels of correlation (from -1.0 to +1.0) between assets one and two are shown. The option to switch in this case is clearly affected not only by the rising project volatility but also in the case of changing correlation coefficient between the two design alternatives. In the case of $\rho_{12} = +1.0$ there is no noteworthy difference to a point-based development process. The reason is that both design mimic each other perfectly and therefore basically behave as one design alternative. Though, as the correlation coefficient changes from +1.0 towards -1.0 the option value is increased significantly. In other words, there is a 'portfolio effect' in the case of set-based development. The economical interpretation of changing correlation coefficients can be made in terms of exploration of the design space and varying marketing concepts. If the two design alternatives are derived from dissimilar technical approaches and are aimed at different market circumstances the correlation coefficient can be expected to decrease. Because management has the flexibility at the end of the development phase to choose the best project the automotive design can be expected to be significantly more mature. In financial terms this is expressed in terms of a markedly higher option value.

Figure 42: The Effect of Relative Volatility with Two Design Alternatives

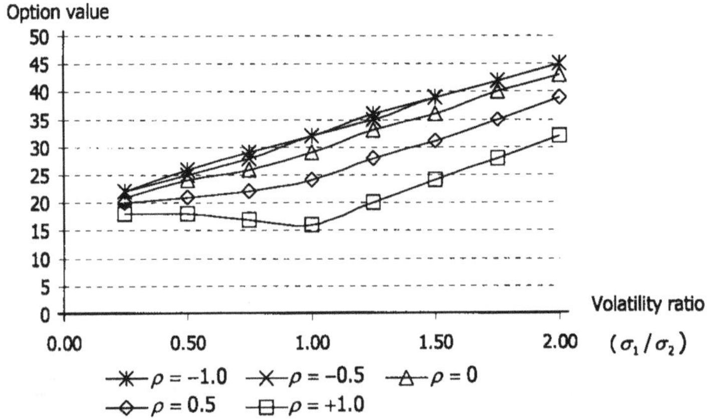

Data: $\sigma_2 = 0.4$, $S_1 = S_2 = 100$, $X = 100$, $T = 1$, $N = 2$, $r_f = 0.05$

Source: own creation, see also Appendix 4

Figure 42 demonstrates the effect of design alternatives with differing volatilities. When the volatility of design alternative one is low (= low volatility ratio) the option value is dominated by asset two. The situation changes once the volatility ratio increases. When the volatility ratio is above 1.5 the option value is derived primarily from design alternative one because this design alternative has a higher probability of being implemented. Though, irrespective of the volatility ratio the option value with two design alternatives is still higher than point-based development alternative (in Figure 40). Again, the the correlation coefficient plays an important role in determining the value of the development process.

Figure 43: The Effect of the Underlying Values with Two Design Alternatives

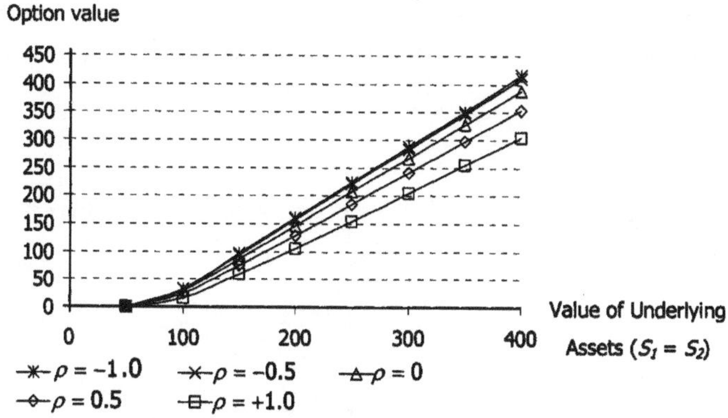

Data: $\sigma_1 = \sigma_2 = 0.4$, $X = 100$, $T = 1$, $N = 2$, $r_f = 0.05$

Source: own creation, see also Appendix 4

Figure 43 depicts the increase in option value when the current value of each design alternative increases. Clearly some of the highest option values are achieved in this manner. Particularly, if $\rho_{12} < 0$, $S_1 > 350$, and $S_2 > 350$ then the option value is at least as high as the current value of the underlying. That is, the option value in effect doubles the ENPV of the development process. The greater starting values for the design alternatives in the lattice result in a high probability for very large values of the underlying design alternatives and consequently for the designs being implemented. Though for higher starting values, compared with the point-based development process in Figure 40 the difference is rather small. This is due to the fact that management does not need to develop two designs when there is high probability of a point-based development yielding an above-average outcome. As is the case in the previous figures, the correlation coefficient in Figure 43 is an important determinant for the value of the development process. E.g., with the underlying values at 400, going from +1 to -1 correlation increases the value of the development project by more than 33%. I.e., a substantial increase in value is to be expected if it is possible to find underlying values, which have less than perfect positive correlation.

Figure 44: The Effect of Relative Project Value with Two Design Alternatives

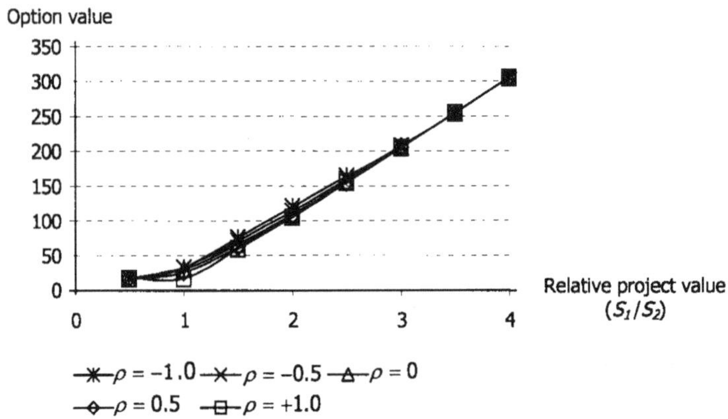

Data: $S_2 = 100$, $\sigma_1 = \sigma_2 = 0.4$, $X = 100$, $T = 1$, $N = 2$, $r_f = 0.05$

Source: own creation, see also Appendix 4

Figure 44 illustrates the growth in the option value when design alternative one becomes increasingly valuable relative to design alternative two. The probability of design alternative one being implemented quickly surpasses that of design alternative two. As a result the option value is due to the high starting value of design alternative one. Consequently, the difference to the option value in a point-based development process is small because it never becomes optimal to switch to design alternative two.

Figure 45: The Effect of Project Volatility with Three Design Alternatives

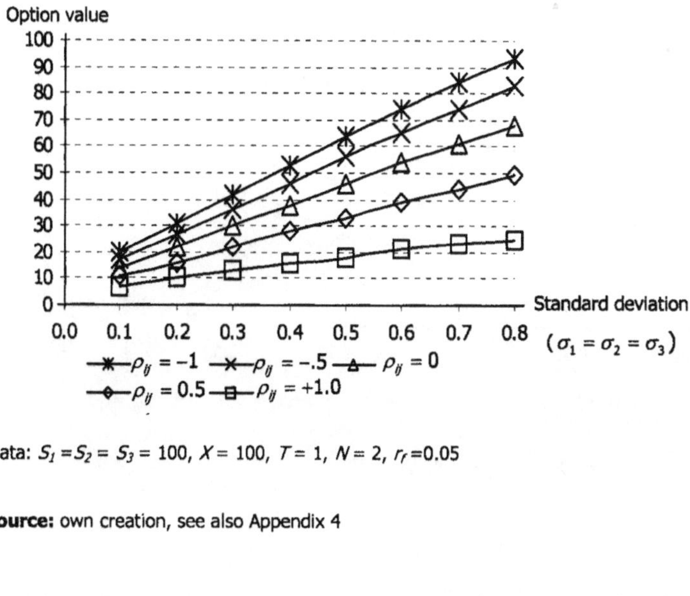

Data: $S_1 = S_2 = S_3 = 100$, $X = 100$, $T = 1$, $N = 2$, $r_f = 0.05$

Source: own creation, see also Appendix 4

Figure 45 shows the effect of increasing volatility on the option value in a set-based development process with three design alternatives. In the case of perfect positive correlation there is basically no difference to a point-based development process. The reason is identical to the case of perfect positive correlation in the set-based development of two design alternatives. Still, as the standard deviations of the design alternatives increase the option value increases linearly. A set-based development process therefore becomes very valuable when there are higher degrees of volatility and lower levels of correlation. The management perspective is clear. It shoould focus on design alternatives, which are different in technical and market terms, at the beginning of the development process. This has a tremendous impact on the resulting value of the option to switch. In the case of 0.8 volatility the option value increases roughly 300% when the design alternatives go from +1 to -1 correlation.

Figure 46: The Effect of Relative Project Volatility with Three Design Alternatives

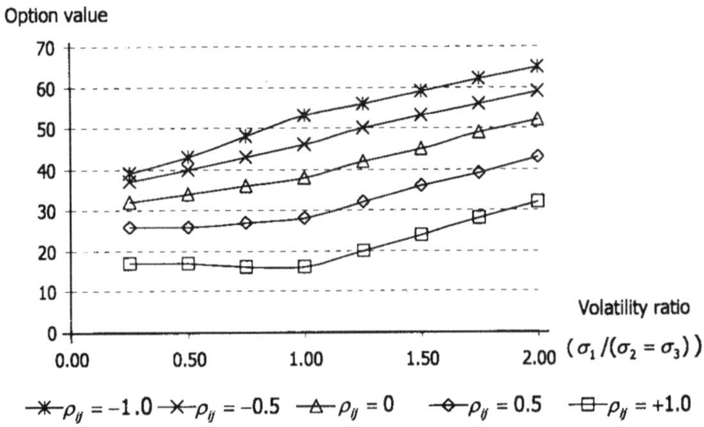

Data: $S_1 = S_2 = S_3 = 100$, $X = 100$, $T = 1$, $N = 2$, $r_f = 0.05$

Source: own creation, see also Appendix 4

Figure 46 shows an increase in option value compared to the two-design case in Figure 42. Again, the requirement is that the design alternatives do not have a perfect positive correlation, in which case there is no value-added of developing sets concurrently (compare with the option values in Figure 40).

Figure 47: The Effect of the Underlying Values with Three Design Alternatives

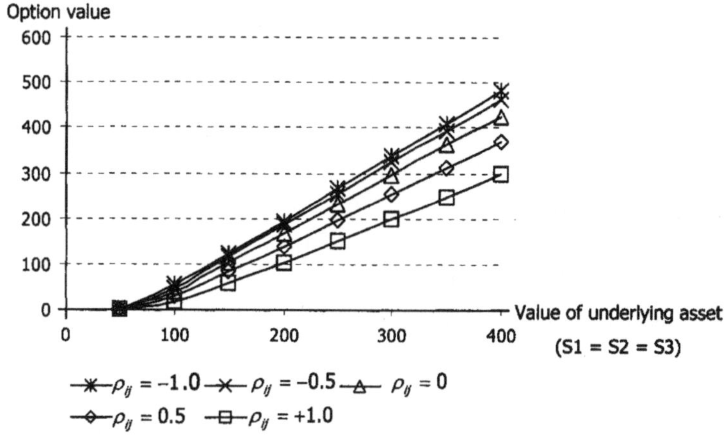

Data: $\sigma_1 = \sigma_2 = \sigma_3 = 0.4$, $X = 100$, $T = 1$, $N = 2$, $r_f = 0.05$

Source: own creation, see also Appendix 4

Compared to the case in Figure 43 the development of three design alternatives in parallel shows a clear increase in option value for design alternatives, which have less than perfect positive correlation (i.e., $\rho_{ij} < +1.0$). The resulting option values now quickly surpass the value of the underlying design alternatives. Once again, the value of the option to switch between design alternatives makes up a significant part of the value of the automobile development process.

5.2 Deriving an Optimal Development Process Setup

The following sections shall be devoted to a direct comparison of the point- and set-based models of automotive development. The objective is to determine an optimal development process setup.

5.2.1 The Option Value of the Number of Design Alternatives

Figure 18 illustrated a trade-off between the value of the option to switch and the development costs. This trade-off is modelled and subsequently solved for an optimal number of design alternatives.

Figure 48: The Effect of the Number of Underlyings and their Volatilities on the Option Value

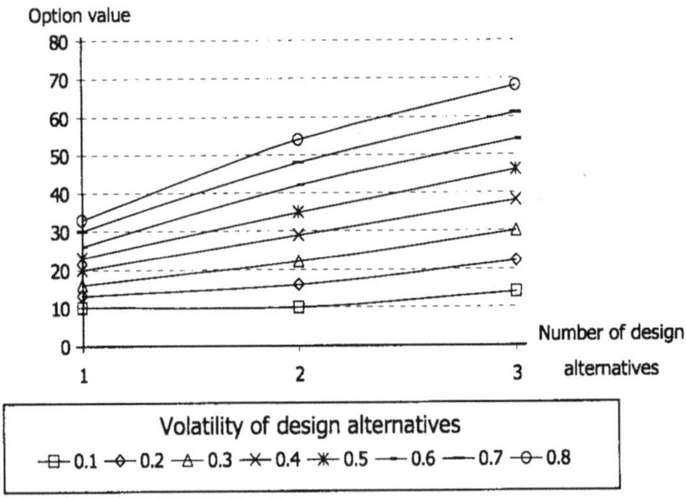

Data: $S_1 = S_2 = S_3 = 100$, $\rho_{12} = \rho_{13} = \rho_{23} = 0$, $X = 100$, $T = 1$, $N = 2$, $r_f = 0.05$

Source: own creation, see also Appendix 4

Figure 48 depicts an increasing option value when then number of design alternatives being developed concurrently increases. I.e., a set-based development process has a higher option value as long as there is uncertainty about the future value of the respective design alternatives. E.g., if the volatility is 0.8 then the option value increases roughly by 100% when management chooses to develop in a set-based manner (n = 3) instead of developing in a point-based manner (n = 1).

Figure 49: The Effect of the Number of Underlyings and Their Values on the Option Value

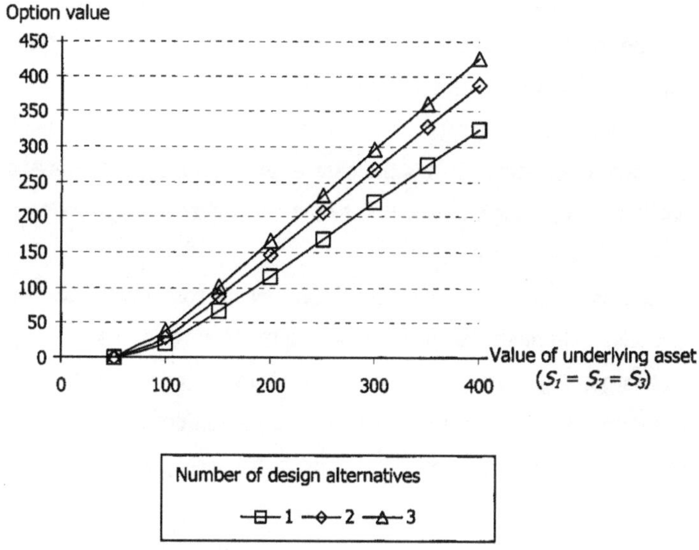

Data: $\sigma_1 = \sigma_2 = \sigma_3 = 0.4$, $\rho_{12} = \rho_{13} = \rho_{23} = 0$, $X = 100$, $T = 1$, $N = 2$, $r_f = 0.05$

Source: own creation, see also Appendix 4

Figure 49 recapitulates the previous results that the values of the underlying assets generally increase option value. In addition Figure 49 clearly shows the value-added of developing in sets.

5.2.2 The Optimal Development Process Setup: Linear Cost Structure

Thus far the focus has been on computing the option value in different development process settings. In order to find the ENPV one must additionally subtract the upfront development process investment costs. This is the before mentioned trade-off between the option value and the development process investment costs. It is the goal of management to structure the development process in such a way that the value of the option to switch is greater than the thereby related development process investment costs. Two types of development process costs structures are considered as characteristic for the automotive development processes in general:

1) The first is a linear cost structure. I.e., the development costs rise linearly with the number of design alternatives. This is the case when the variable costs associated with the automobile development increase due to the extra needed engineering hours, dies for prototype constructions, etc..

2) The second is a cost structure influenced by a cost multiplier. That is, the development costs rise more than linearly due to capacity restraints and organizational limitations at large. E.g., increasing the set-size leads to certain inefficiencies, which make it increasingly prohibitive for the developing organization to work concurrently.

An example of a linear development process cost structure is given in Figure 50.

Figure 50: Automotive Development with a Linear Cost Structure

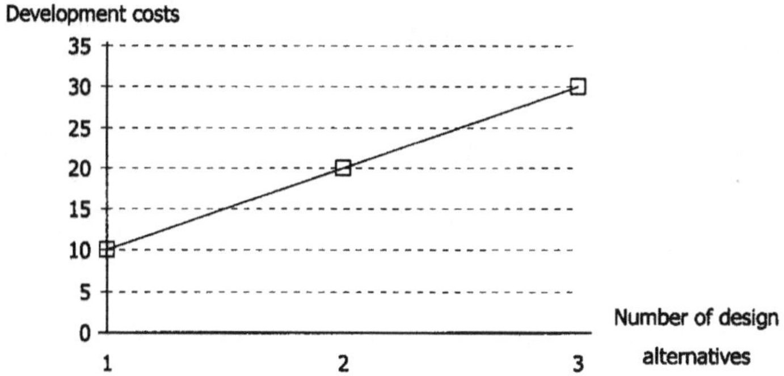

Development costs = $n \bullet 10$

Source: own creation

Figure 51 shows the option values for the number of design alternatives developed in parallel and their correlation coefficients.

Figure 51: The Effect of the Number of Underlyings on the Option Value

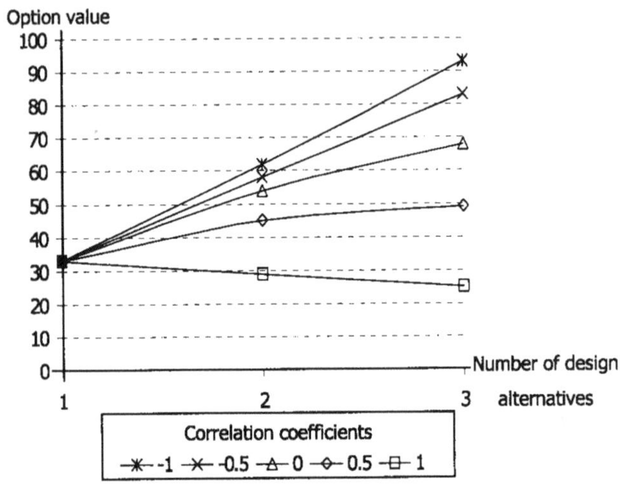

Data: $S_1 = S_2 = S_3 = 100$, $\sigma_1 = \sigma_2 = \sigma_3 = 0.8$, $X = 100$, $T = 1$, $N = 2$, $r_f = 0.05$

Source: own creation, see also Appendix 4

In order to find the ENVP of the development process the linear costs structure in Figure 50 is subtracted from the option values in Figure 51. The result is shown in Figure 52.

Figure 52: ENPV as a Function of the Development Process – Linear Costs

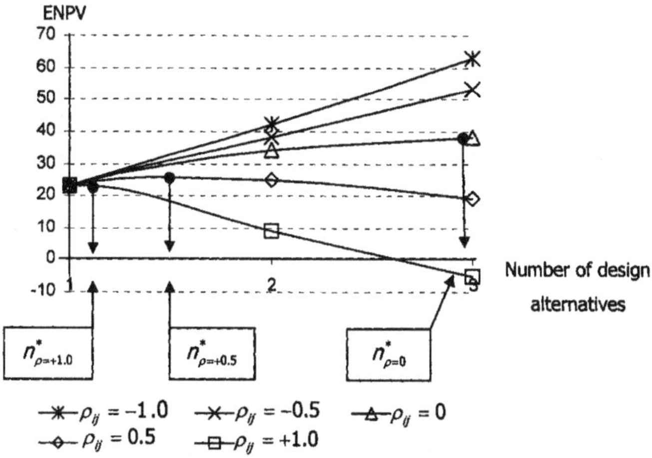

n^* = the optimal number of designs to developed concurrently

Data: $S_1 = S_2 = S_3 = 100$, $\sigma_1 = \sigma_2 = \sigma_3 = 0.8$, $X = 100$, $T = 1$, $N = 2$, $r_f = 0.05$

Source: own creation, see also Appendix 4

It is now possible to present the optimal number of design alternatives, which is determined by the point on the ENPV curve where it has its maximum. For ρ_{ij} = -1.0 and ρ_{ij} = -0.5 the optimum lies somewhere in the range n > 3. For ρ_{ij} = 0 the maximum is at n = 3. That is to say, given the specific data utilized in Figure 52, management should develop three design alternatives in parallel. This specific development process setup maximizes the ENPV. For ρ_{ij} = 0.5 the optimum lies at between one and two design alternatives being developed. For the case when ρ_{ij} = +1.0 management should clearly choose a point-based development process. A set-based development process would in this case destroy value. The reason is the perfect mimicking of the design alternatives. There is therefore no value-added exploration of the design space.

5.2.3 The Optimal Development Process Setup: Non-Linear Cost Structure

Figure 53 shows the case of a non-linear development process cost structure.

Figure 53: Automotive Development with a Non-Linear Cost Structure

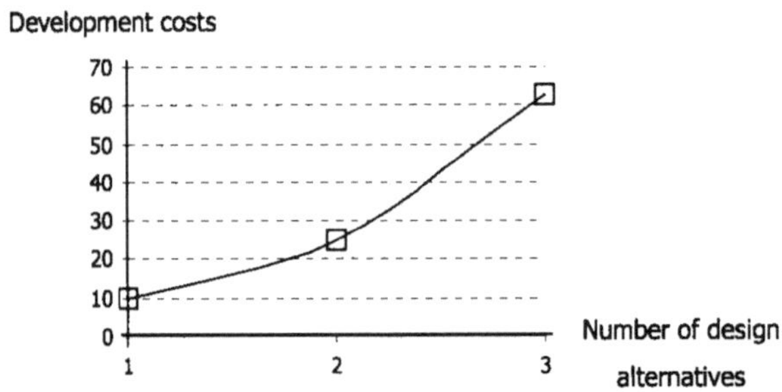

Cost multiplier = 50%

Development costs:

$n = 1$: $\underline{-10}$

$n = 2$: $-10 - (10 \times (1+\text{cost multiplier})) = \underline{-25}$

$n = 3$: $-25 - (25 \times (1+\text{cost multiplier})) = \underline{-62.5}$

Source: own creation

The variable costs of developing multiple design alternatives in parallel in the above example increase according to an arbitrarily chosen cost multiplier (50% in the case above). The net effect is a stronger limitation of the development efforts, which the automotive company can undertake. The resulting ENPV with non-linear development costs is illustrated in Figure 54.

Figure 54: ENPV as a Function of the Development Process – Non-Linear Costs

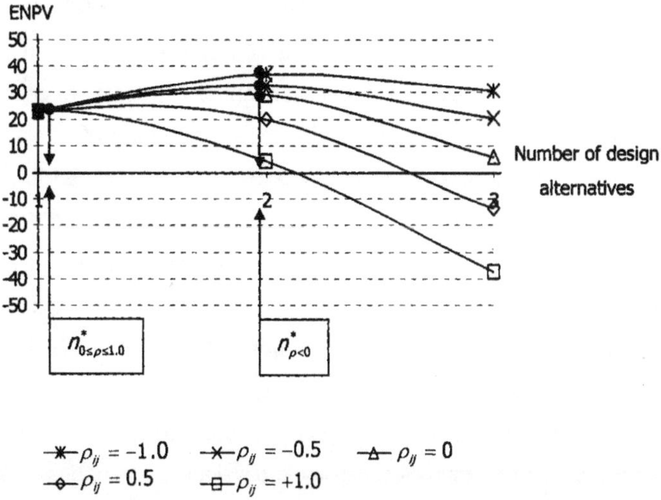

Data: $S_1 = S_2 = S_3 = 100$, $\sigma_1 = \sigma_2 = \sigma_3 = 0.8$, $X = 100$, $T = 1$, $N = 2$, $r_f = 0.05$

Source: own creation, see also Appendix 4

Compared to Figure 52, the non-linear cost structure has reduced the optimal number of design alternatives to be developed in parallel. The option value of developing many design alternatives in parallel is less than the thereby incurred development process costs. In other words, it is too expensive to develop many design alternatives in parallel. For $-1.0 \le \rho_{ij} \le 0$ the optimal number of designs to develop concurrently is roughly $n = 2$.

For design alternatives with positive correlation coefficient the optimal number of designs is less, namely, $n = 1$.

5.3 Five Principles of Automotive Development

The purpose of the following sections is to establish a set of general indicators to support the choice of an automotive development process setup. Based on the thesis thus far it is possible to identify five principles of automotive development, which are presented and discussed.

5.3.1 Capabilities in Platform Design and Developing Sets Concurrently

The first principle of automotive development is: Capabilities in platform design and developing sets concurrently induce set-based development. In order to develop sets of design alternatives concurrently it is essential to have some form of modularity in the automotive product architecture. Modularity makes it technically feasible to switch between design alternatives. The value of the option to switch is in turn determined by the organizational capability in platform development (systems engineering), e.g., in the case at Toyota. The overall architecture sets the limitations for the exploration of the design space. A poorly designed product platform will most likely yield no valuable exploration of the design space. A lacking capability in platform development will result in an automotive development process reminiscent of the point-based model.

Equally important is an organizational capability in developing sets of design alternatives concurrently. Lack of such a capability is most likely a major hindrance to set-based development in the automobile industry. I.e., the companies, which posses such a capability, will earn rents due to the substantial difficulty in duplicating such a complex knowledge resource. A lacking capability in developing sets of design alternatives concurrently will also result in an automotive development process reminiscent of the point-based model.

5.3.2 Volatility

The second principle of automotive development is: Higher volatility induces set-based development. As the volatility of the individual design alternatives rises so does the value of the option to switch. This result concerning the effect of volatility parallels results from the option pricing literature in general. When the automotive company is faced with higher levels of technical and market uncertainties it should develop larger sets of design alternatives concurrently. E.g., this is the case when uncertainty surrounds the viability of new technologies or uncertainty exists about upcoming environmental regulations. These uncertainties drive the option value because they effect the FCFs from the automobile and thereby the expected value of the automobile.

As the volatility of the individual design alternatives diminishes so does the value of the option to switch. When the automotive developing company is faced with lower levels of technical and market uncertainties it should develop smaller sets of design alternatives concurrently. E.g., this is the case when little uncertainty surrounds the viability of the employed technologies or when the market situation is characterized by stability. The extreme case of zero volatility induces a strictly point-based automotive development process.

5.3.3 Correlation

The third principle of automotive development is: Lower levels of correlation induce set-based development. The value of the option to switch increases when the correlation coefficient decreases. This corresponds to a broader exploration of the design space from both a technical and a market perspective. Lower levels of correlation characterize designs, which have high values in different scenarios of the world. The automotive company in effect immunizes itself towards technical and market volatility (uncertainty) by developing larger sets concurrently. This is a key result of this thesis and may be labelled: the portfolio effect in automotive development.

5.3.4 Dominant Design Alternatives

The fourth principle of automotive development is: Dominant design alternatives induce point-based development. A design alternative is dominant if the PV of its expected FCFs significantly exceeds the implementation costs (i.e., the design alternative has a high NPV). In this case the automotive developing company should develop a smaller set of design alternatives in parallel. E.g., if a certain technology has proven itself within and outside of the company for years, and no other design alternative has a similar NPV, it makes no sense for the developing company to develop large sets concurrently.

If no design alternative is dominant (i.e., all the design alternatives similarly have an NPV close to zero), the automotive developing company should develop larger sets of design alternatives in parallel. In this case there are no obviously valuable design alternatives available, and it makes sense to try and develop better design alternatives.

5.3.5 Capabilities to Manage Competent Suppliers

The fifth principle of automotive development is: Capabilities to manage competent suppliers induce set-based development. The core economic argument is that of specialization (comparative advantage), which enables sustainable improvements in the product benefits and the product cost structure. In the case of linear development costs the value of the option to switch increases with the number of design alternatives. I.e., the development costs are kept at low levels even though a more extensive exploration of the design space takes place. Equivalently, the overall degree of efficiency is high even when the number of designs being developed concurrently is high. This is characteristic for longer-standing partnerships in the automotive industry, e.g., in the case of Toyota, and requires a capability in working with competent suppliers in all stages of the automotive product lifecycle.

In the case of non-linear development costs the optimal number of design alternatives is reduced dramatically. This is characteristic for a development process where there are constraints to exploring the design space more extensively. E.g., development costs increase significantly if enlarging the set of design alternatives results in a certain degree of confusion and decreasing overall efficiency.

5.4 Model Criticism and Future Research

This section is concerned with the subjects of model criticism and a discussion of future research possibilities. First, the utilized methodology and the applied analyses are discussed from a scientific standpoint concerning their validity. This is an important task, which has the purpose of dealing with the impacts of the utilized assumptions and models. Second, based on the results in this work, possible future research areas are identified and discussed. The purpose here is to show where there likely exists promising fields for further research.

5.4.1 Model Criticism

The following points have been identified by the author and will be briefly mentioned and discussed in the following:

1) The preceding real options model didn't incorporate any effects arising from competitors. One would assume that the identified option value within the development process is dependent on the behaviour of the developing company's competitors. E.g., in the case of cleaner air technologies for automobiles, the introduction of a next generation technology by a competitor in the market would likely mean an upward movement in regulation, which in turn would necessitate a corresponding implementation by the developing company. In general, the existence of competitors has the same effect as dividends have on American options (Trigeorgis 1991). I.e., the timing and value of the investment is influenced by competition. An explicit modelling of competition in an options framework can be accomplished by utilizing game-theoretic principles from industrial organization (see Smit and Ankum 1993 and Smit and Trigeorgis 2006).

2) In practice there is an interdependence between the product development process and the production process. This was discussed in Chapter 2. Though, the preceding real options model didn't explicitly model this interdependence. E.g., a change in the production process would likely have an effect on the value of a given design alternative. I.e., there are simultaneously existing real options on the same underlying (the product) in both the development and production processes. A more realistic model would explicitly model managerial flexibility in the production process and subsequently implement a dynamic recursive optimization of the value of the product for both sets of options.

3) The validity of the employed secondary data is a critical aspect of this work. This concerns particularly the results presented by Clark and Fujimoto (1991) and Sobek

(1997) in the course of their empirical research within the global automotive industry and the development process at Toyota respectively. The structures and further analyses of the automotive development process presented in this work are to a great extent based on the data and observations made in the mentioned sources. It has been shown that the automotive development process is a very complex object to study. With this in mind, any researcher undertaking empirical research with the objective of identifying the key causalities existing in the various companies is confronted with the complexity and ambiguity of the process of innovation. This must be taken into consideration when evaluating the results from the empirical work.

4) The operazionalization of the term capability in practice presents a formidable challenge for any research concerned with identifying and measuring key business processes in connection with the automobile development process. This point was discussed briefly in the context of chapter 3. Further, the various components of the development process at Toyota where linked to specific capabilities. This primarily affects the reliability of the approach, given specific empirical data and the models from the RBV.

5) The use of models from financial economics to the analysis of real assets presents several challenges, which must be taken into consideration when viewing the results.
First, the analysis in chapter 5 is based on the assumption of incomplete financial markets, which is a realistic assumption. Though, it is important to remember that the owner(s) of the developing company were assumed to be risk-neutral towards private risks. If this were not the case, there no longer exists a unique martingale measure. Rather, a set of possible martingale measures now exist, and this leads to a specification of option values in intervals.
Second, the analysis in this work was based on the assumption that the identified capabilities can be modelled using a real option to switch. Capabilities include much managerial flexibility, and therefore other real options might also be identified. The values of these shadow options where not explicitly calculated and taken into account.

Nonetheless, if imbedded in the analysis, they would invariably increase the calculated value of the automobile development process. This would in turn lead to a marginal increase in the optimal size of the set to develop concurrently due to the relative increase in the option value component compared to the investment cost component.

Third, the analysis in chapter 5 applied a numerical approximation technique. It must therefore be taken into consideration that the "true" option values are only achieved by a very large number of steps in the lattice. In contrast, the applied lattice used only a small number of steps in calculating the option value of the multivariate contingent claim. There is therefore inevitably an approximation error contained in the results shown in this work.

Fourth, the analyses in this work applied a neoclassic approach to the valuation of the automobile development process. The informational economics view was mentioned and briefly discussed but it was not part of the following analysis and consequently doesn't show up in the calculated results. Recent theoretical research in the field of investment timing and an explicit modelling of behavioural uncertainty has shown that the ensuing investment timing is either too early or too late compared to the base case (neoclassic) approach (see Grenadier and Wang 2004).

5.4.2 Future Research

This section concerns possible future research areas, which can be considered based on the results of this thesis:

1) Empirical research could be undertaken in order to examine the following aspects:

First, within the frame of the automotive development process, a methodology for identifying capabilities could be developed based on primary data. The purpose would be to increase the reliability of the overall approach when working with capabilities. Such a methodology would also be of interest for the general field of empirical research employing the models from strategic management and would be in line with recent research in the field of strategic management (Brown and Duguid 2001).

Second, one or more automotive developing companies could be selected in order to gather primary data, yielding further insights into the determinants of successful development systems. These companies should be characterized by the existence of managerial flexibility and an uncertain technical and market environment. As it was shown, these are some of the key value drivers for the automotive development process. In particular, as discussed by Sobek (1997) in his research at Toyota, data should be gathered, which supply information about the actual management of the development funnel, i.e., the process of opening up and subsequently narrowing the funnel, as this information is a central input to the subsequent valuation and optimization of the investment process.

2) Research needs to be undertaken to model explicitly and quantatively the impact of behavioural uncertainty on the automobile development process. There is still much potential in the academic literature, in particular in the valuation of contingent claims, to try to merge the neoclassic and informational economics perspectives in the valuation of real assets (Grenadier and Wang 2004). Significant behavioural uncertainties would have to be identified empirically, and subsequent quantification of these uncertainties should be attempted employing various cooperative contract designs in order to maximize the value of the development process.

5.5 Chapter Summary

This chapter dealt with identifying an optimal setup for the development process. In doing so, five principles of automotive development where identified. The BEG model was utilized in order to compute the effect of interactions between design alternatives on the value of the automotive development process. The results were substantiated by both empirical findings from major automotive developing companies and a resource-based analysis of the automotive development process. The five principles to optimizing the automotive development process are summarized in the following.

The first principle argues for the importance of a capability in platform design combined with the capability to work efficiently with sets in parallel. I.e., the value of the option to switch can only be attained, once the automotive company possesses the needed capabilities. The second principle pertains to the effect of volatility on the development process setup. As technical and market uncertainties rise so does the optimal number of design alternatives to be developed concurrently. The third principle deals with the level of correlation between the design alternatives. In the case of perfect positive correlation management should employ a point-based development process, because the various design alternatives only mimic each other. Once the level of correlation diminishes the optimal number of design alternatives to be developed concurrently increases, because each design alternative now represents a potentially valuable solution to specific states of the world. The fourth principle states that the existence of a dominant design alternative reduces the optimal size of the set to be developed concurrently. The dominant design alternative is superior, compared to the other alternatives, and has a high probability of being implemented. Consequently, there is no need for an extensive exploration of the design space. The fifth principle deals with the supplier relationship and states that management should seek to build up and sustain relationships with competent suppliers in order to gain access to their unique resources and capabilities. This access allows for lower cost exploration of the design space and subsequently a more extensive exploration of the design space.

Given the five proposed design principles and the quantitative valuation model of the automotive development process it is possible to give specific recommendations to management in order to optimize the value of the development process. It is important to notice that value of the option to switch is generated by very specific and unique capabilities. Management should be aware of the circumstances when these capabilities are of value.

It was shown that it is not always optimal to develop large sets concurrently. This is the case when: the organization possesses no capability in developing a product platform and no capability in developing sets of design alternatives in parallel; there is little uncertainty; potential design alternatives have a high level of positive correlation; a superior design alternative exists; and there are no extensive relationships with competent suppliers. In some circumstances it is optimal to develop larger sets of design alternatives concurrently. This is the case when: the organization possesses a capability in developing a product platform and a capability in developing sets of design alternatives in parallel; there is much uncertainty; potential design alternatives have little positive correlation; no superior design alternative exists; and there are extensive relationships with competent suppliers.

Finally, this chapter presented a critique of the presented valuation model and some perspectives for future research possibilities. In particular, the incorporating the effects of competition and an explicit modelling of the simultaneous development and production processes would be of value. Furthermore, there is a need in literature for a clear and methodologically sound approach to identifying and arguing for the specific real options to be focused on in a given practical setting. Future research in this area could be undertaken by merging the real options framework with the models of strategic management.

Chapter 6: Conclusion

The following sections present the answers to the problems in the problem statement.

6.1 Subproblem 1

Chapter 2 dealt with the automobile, the structure and function of automotive development, and three different ways of developing an automobile. Categorized as a product, the automobile can be characterized by high degrees of product complexity both internally and externally. The challenge for the developing company is to develop the automobile in a timely manner while achieving high levels of productivity and integrity.

A key result concerning the automotive development process is the role of information about the technical and market prospects of the automobile. The focus on the physical product as such becomes secondary to the information resulting from the unfolding uncertainties surrounding the development effort. An essential element in generating information about the uncertainties is the exploration of the design space through well directed design-build-test cycles employing prototypes as information generating vehicles. Consequently management should place their emphasis on the way prototypes of design alternatives are employed in order to explore the design space.

Chapter 2.3 presented three models of automotive development, which were introduced by means of an example: finding an optimal meeting time. The simplest development model is point-based serial engineering. According to this model management chooses the current most optimal design and develops it through several sequential iterative cycles. The second model is point-based concurrent engineering. It also chooses the current most optimal design for development. However, it is developed employing concurrent feedback cycles from all participating development functions and as such presents a logical optimization of the serial development process. The third and final development model is set-based concurrent engineering. The differences to point-based concurrent engineering consist in the size of the set of design alternatives developed in parallel and the implicit notion of a modular product architecture. The concept of a development funnel was applied to illustrate the managerial effects of set-based development. It was shown that there are two main managerial implications pertaining to managing the development funnel: opening the mouth of the funnel and killing non-optimal design alternatives. Finally, in chapter 2.4 the point- and set-based models of concurrent engineering were compared according to their performance on the important dimensions of: exploration of the design space, level of integration, investment costs, accommodation of uncertainty, and managerial flexibilities provided. Based on these performance criteria, a trade-off was identified between a more extensive exploration of the design space and the higher investment costs associated with developing more than one design alternative in parallel. This trade-off is modelled explicitly in chapter 4, and chapter 5 presents numerical examples of how to determine an optimal size of the set of design alternatives to develop in parallel.

6.2 Subproblem 2

Chapter 3 dealt with how an organization attains a competitive advantage. The literature proposes two main groups of models to solve this problem: strategic fit and strategic stretch. The first group, industry structural analysis, focuses primarily on the external environment of the organization and *where* the organization should choose to compete. The second group, RBV, focuses mainly on the internal environment of the organization and *how* the organization should choose to compete.

The central tenet of the RBV is that an organization achieves Ricardian rents resulting from market imperfections due to firm-level efficiency advantage(s) in meeting the CSFs better than the competition. There exist two components of this efficiency advantage: resources and capabilities. Both are unique and cannot be copied or acquired easily by the competition, thereby fortifying the advantage.

Of particular importance are the capabilities because they represent complex knowledge resources. As was also the case in chapter 2, information is at the core of the process of sequential choice. An organization's potential to apply and develop its capabilities is determined by its absorptive capacity, which determines how the organization learns. The most basic form of learning is single-loop learning and occurs when an organization exercises its flexibility. The more advanced form of learning is labelled double-loop learning and takes place when an organization learns about the way it learns. Double-loop learning therefore implies a compounding effect in the process of sequential choice. It is purposeful to classify capabilities according to two categories: component capabilities and architectural capabilities. Component capabilities are individual firm-specific business processes. Architectural capabilities employ and develop the component capabilities. I.e., architectural capabilities have a platform property, which can also be utilized in working with suppliers in order to gain access to their capabilities. Consequently, the RBV views resources as the building blocks of component capabilities, and component capabilities as the building blocks of architectural capabilities.

Based on empirical research undertaken in the automobile industry, it is possible to identify two archetypes of automotive development processes. The first archetype has a focused mouth and practices a fast narrowing of the development funnel. This system may be considered a derivative of the point-based concurrent development process. It is observed frequently in the US and Europe. The focus is on technical aspects of the prototype developed. The development process is traditionally functional in nature and results in lower degrees of internal and external integration. The second archetype has a wide mouth and carries out a slow narrowing of the development funnel. This system may be considered a derivative of the set-based concurrent development process. It is observed frequently in Japan. The focus is on the prototype as an information-generating vehicle to be utilized as part of the organizational learning process. The development process is typically cross-functional in nature and results in higher degrees of internal and external integration.

The empirical results therefore raise the issue of whether an automotive developer can achieve a competitive advantage through the use of a wider development funnel, i.e., by increasing the set of design alternatives being developed concurrently. An important aspect of widening the development funnel was the observed use of suppliers in the early stages of the development process. This was especially the case in Japan and at Toyota in particular.

Finally, the automotive development process at Toyota was considered as being representative of the set-based approach and analysed in detail. Based upon the empirical research undertaken at Toyota in Japan it was possible to identify several unique resources and capabilities as applied within Toyota's development process. The capabilities were subsequently ranked, and the result was the identification of three component capabilities as well as four architectural capabilities.

6.3 Subproblem 3

The first part of chapter 4 dealt with the role of financial markets in valuing the automotive development process. The so-called discipline of the financial markets states that the prices of marketed securities contain information relevant to the valuation of corporate strategy. It is possible to explain the firm-specific efficiency advantage(s) utilizing a real option valuation model. The utilized approach is to model the corporate decision-making process as resulting in a series of FCFs to be included in a valuation model. Underlying a valuation of the automotive development process is the concept of finding comparable marketed securities, which duplicate the payoffs from the development process. The limitation to this method is given by the open systems nature of strategic management, which makes it difficult to model quantitatively all aspects of the process of sequential choice. Given simplifying arguments it is possible to model the essential causalities in terms of a real option model. Maximizing the value of this model implies finding an optimal automotive development process setup.

The second part of chapter 4 presented a general valuation framework, with which any claim can be valued. Assuming no-arbitrage and given complete markets it was shown that there exists a unique equivalent martingale measure. The value of a given claim thus equals the expected, discounted value of the claim taken with respect to the martingale measure. Equivalently, if the market price of risk is known, it was shown that the martingale approach (CCA) coincides with the value found using DP. In the case of incomplete markets there exist private risks, which aren't spanned by the prices of marketed securities. This is most likely the case in automotive development when unique capabilities (which per definition cannot be duplicated) give rise to payoff structures. There no longer exists a unique martingale measure, and any duplication of payoffs resulting from the automotive development process now results in a tracking error. In order to value the private risks, an assumption is needed regarding the risk-preference of the owners of the automotive developing company towards the private risks. In this thesis they are presumed risk-neutral towards private risks.

The third part of chapter 4 briefly gave an overview of option valuation techniques. The focus in this thesis is on identifying the relevant real options for the valuation of the automotive development process. To this purpose the previous analysis of the capabilities in Toyota's automotive development process was taken as a starting point. The option to switch was chosen as the most dominant real option existing within a given automotive development project. This is in concurrence with the observation of development funnels in practice: Widening the mouth of the development funnel ensures a choice between more design alternatives. The value of this option to choose (switch) is driven by the values of the n underlying design alternatives. The strategic problem to solve is therefore how to determine the size (n) of the initial set of design alternatives to be developed.

The fourth part of chapter 4 presented the BEG model. The option to choose between the n design alternatives is modelled as a multivariate contingent claim. For illustrative purposes, the set size was limited to a maximum of $n = 3$. The equivalent martingale measure was computed in the cases on $n = 2$ and $n = 3$. The resulting lattices were shown in the cases of $n = 1$, $n = 2$, and $n = 3$. Finally, the cash flow structures to be applied in the real option model were shown for $n = 1$, $n = 2$, and $n = 3$.

6.4 Subproblem 4

Chapter 5 dealt with identifying an optimal setup for the development process. In doing so, five principles of automotive development process where identified. The BEG model was utilized in order to compute the effect of interactions between design alternatives on the value of the automotive development process. The results were substantiated by both empirical findings from major automotive developing companies and a resource-based analysis of the automotive development process. The five principles to optimizing the automotive development process are summarized in the following.

The first principle argues for the importance of a capability in platform design combined with the capability to work efficiently with sets in parallel. I.e., the value of the option to switch can only be attained, once the automotive company possesses the needed capabilities. The second principle pertains to the effect of volatility on the development process setup. As technical and market uncertainties rise so does the optimal number of design alternatives to be developed concurrently. The third principle deals with the level of correlation between the design alternatives. In the case of perfect positive correlation management should employ a point-based development process, because the various design alternatives only mimic each other. Once the level of correlation diminishes the optimal number of design alternatives to be developed concurrently increases, because each design alternative now represents a potentially valuable solution to specific states of the world. The fourth principle states that the existence of a dominant design alternative reduces the optimal size of the set to be developed concurrently. The dominant design alternative is superior, compared to the other alternatives, and has a high probability of being implemented. Consequently, there is no need for an extensive exploration of the design space. The fifth principle deals with the supplier relationship and states that management should seek to build up and sustain relationships with competent suppliers in order to gain access to their unique resources and capabilities. This access allows for lower cost exploration of the design space and subsequently a more extensive exploration of the design space.

Given the five proposed design principles and the quantitative valuation model of the automotive development process it is possible to give specific recommendations to management in order to optimize the value of the development process. It is important to notice that value of the option to switch is generated by very specific and unique capabilities. Management should be aware of the circumstances when these capabilities are of value.

It was shown that it is not always optimal to develop large sets concurrently. This is the case when: the organization possesses no capability in developing a product platform and no capability in developing sets of design alternatives in parallel; there is little uncertainty; potential design alternatives have a high level of positive correlation; a superior design alternative exists; and there are no extensive relationships with competent suppliers. In some circumstances it is optimal to develop larger sets of design alternatives concurrently. This is the case when: the organization possesses a capability in developing a product platform and a capability in developing sets of design alternatives in parallel; there is much uncertainty; potential design alternatives have little positive correlation; no superior design alternative exists; and there are extensive relationships with competent suppliers.

Finally, Chapter 5 presented a critique of the presented valuation model and some perspectives for future research possibilities. In particular, the incorporating the effects of competition and an explicit modelling of the simultaneous development and production processes would be of value. Furthermore, there is a need in literature for a clear and methodologically sound approach to identifying and arguing for the specific real options to be focused on in a given practical setting. Future research in this area could be undertaken by merging the real options framework with the models of strategic management.

6.5 Chapter Summary

This thesis presented a novel approach to the automobile development process. It consists of three separate pillars: engineering systems analysis, strategic management analysis, and financial economics. A holistic approach was applied to solving to the problem statement.

First, recent research in the worldwide automobile industry as well as research done at Toyota revealed major differences in the ways automobiles were developed. Two dominant development strategies were identified: point-based and set-based concurrent engineering. It was shown that the use of set-based engineering results in a more extensive development process with significant managerial flexibility in an uncertainty technical and market environment. The choice between the point- and set-based development strategies is a decision between incurring higher development costs, in order to achieve a higher value of the managerial flexibility to switch between design alternatives dependent on the uncertain environmental outcomes, and the higher incurred investment costs. In other words, set-based development builds-in managerial flexibility to the development process. This flexibility can be extremely valuable for the developing company.

Second, recent research within the field of strategic management has shown that the way *how* the developing company chooses to develop its cars significantly influences the competitive advantage of the company and thereby its market value. A framework for identifying and analysing firm-level efficiency advantages in terms of resources, capabilities, and dynamic capabilities was introduced and subsequently applied to the empirical findings from the global automotive industry. Particular emphasis was given to the automotive development process at Toyota. The findings supplied evidence for the existence of valuable existing component and architectural capabilities, which were applied in the development process at Toyota.

Third, it was shown that the financial markets contain much information, which can be utilized in order to value and control the automobile development process. The applied neoclassic approach was able to specify the valuation models applicable to the automobile development process. In the case of complete markets the utilized valuation model yields a valuation result given by the existence of a unique martingale measure. In the more realistic case of incomplete markets, results were shown under the assumption of owners, who are risk-averse to market risks and risk-neutral to private (non-market priced) risks. Given these essential assumptions the automobile development process was shown to correspond to a multivariate contingent claim. The underlyings are the expected present values of the free cash flows resulting form each of the design alternatives being developed concurrently. This novel approach allows for a precise quantitative calculation of the optimal size of the development funnel from the viewpoint of the financial markets. Subsequently, the value drivers for the contingent claim where identified and analyzed using a sensitivity analysis. Of particular importance for the results are the volatilities of the market and technical risks, the size of the present values of the design alternatives being developed, the correlation structure between the design alternatives, and the size of the investment costs. In practice there is a need for specific capabilities, which allow management to switch between design alternatives dependent on the uncertain environment. These were capabilities in platform development, managing sets of design alternatives in parallel, knowing when to narrow the development funnel, and supplier management.

The key result of this thesis is that it is possible to calculate precisely the optimal size of the set of design alternatives to be developed concurrently. Finally, in order to aid management in the process of valuing, controlling, and optimizing the automotive development process, five principles of automotive development were proposed.

Appendix

Appendix 1: J.D. Power and Associates 2005 Germany Customer Satisfaction Index (CSI) Study℠

Level of satisfaction of German automobile owners with their car brand

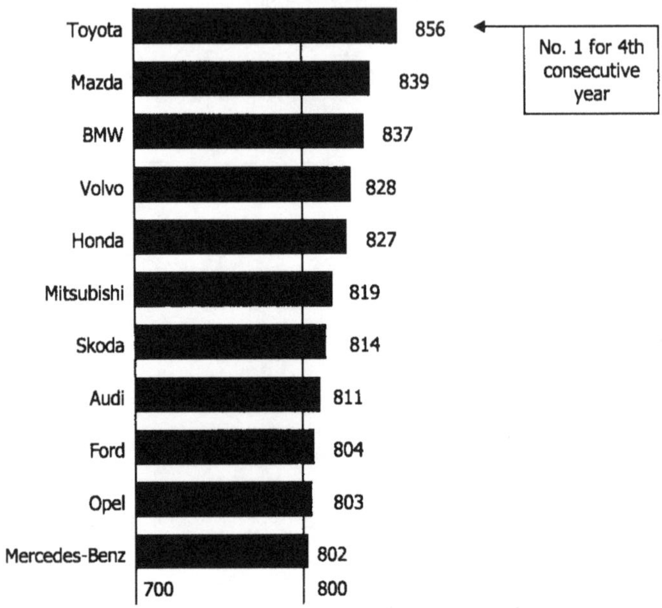

*Based on a 1000-point scale

Source: http://www.jdpower.com/pdf/2005088.pdf (accessed on June 1st 2005)

Appendix 2: Analogy between Financial and Real Options

Financial call	*Real option to invest*	*Affects option value*
Stock price, *S*	Present value of cash flows	+
Strike price, *X*	Investment cost, *I*	-
Time to expiration, *T*	Time to expiration, *T*	+
Volatility, σ	Uncertainty surrounding present value of cash flows	+
Risk-free interest rate, r_f	Risk-free interest rate, r_f	+
Dividends, *DIV*	Missed cash flows from postponing the investment	-

Source: adapted from Hull (2003)

Appendix 3: The Real Option Valuation Process

A six-step process:

1. Develop a list of potential projects or strategies to be evaluated;
2. Conduct a "base case" NPV analysis utilizing time series forecasting to generate static DCF models for each;
3. Apply the DCF results as initial inputs into a Monte Carlo simulation, where volatility and correlations are calculated from the inputs;
4. Frame each project or strategy in terms of real options and focus on the essential real options for further analyses;
5. Compute the real option value using a valuation model (e.g., a binomial lattice);
6. If appropriate, allocate resources within the portfolio of projects.

Source: Mun (2002, p. 322)

Appendix 4: Numerical Results for the BEG Model in Chapter 5

Results for Figure 39: The Effect of Volatility with One Design Alternative

Standard deviation (σ_1)	0.1	0.2	0.3	0.4	0.5	0.6	0.7	0.8
Option value	10	13	16	20	23	26	30	33

Data: $S_1 = 100$, $X = 100$, $T = 1$, $N = 2$, $r_f = 0.05$

Results for Figure 40: The Effect of Underlying Value with One Design Alternative

Underlying Value (S_1)	50	100	150	200	250	300	350	400
Option value	0	20	66	115	168	220	273	325

Data: $\sigma_1 = 0.4$, $X = 100$, $T = 1$, $N = 2$, $r_f = 0.05$

Results for Figure 41: The Effect of Volatility with Two Design Alternatives

	Option value				
$\sigma_1 = \sigma_2$	$\rho = -1.0$	$\rho = -0.5$	$\rho = 0$	$\rho = +0.5$	$\rho = +1.0$
0.1	12	11	10	8	6
0.2	19	18	16	13	10
0.3	26	25	22	18	13
0.4	32	32	29	24	16
0.5	39	39	35	29	20
0.6	45	45	42	34	23
0.7	50	52	48	40	26
0.8	55	58	54	45	29

Data: $S_1 = S_2 = 100$, $X = 100$, $T = 1$, $N = 2$, $r_f = 0.05$

Results for Figure 42: The Effect of Relative Volatility with Two Design Alternatives

	Option value				
σ_1/σ_2	$\rho=-1.0$	$\rho=-0.5$	$\rho=0$	$\rho=+0.5$	$\rho=+1.0$
0.25	22	22	21	20	18
0.50	26	25	24	21	18
0.75	29	28	26	22	17
1.00	32	32	29	24	16
1.25	36	35	33	28	20
1.50	39	39	36	31	24
1.75	42	42	40	35	28
2.00	45	45	43	39	32

Data: $\sigma_2 = 0.4$, $S_1 = S_2 = 100$, $X = 100$, $T = 1$, $N = 2$, $r_f = 0.05$

Results for Figure 43: The Effect of the Underlying Values with Two Design Alternatives

	Option value				
$S_1 = S_2$	$\rho=-1.0$	$\rho=-0.5$	$\rho=0$	$\rho=+0.5$	$\rho=+1.0$
50	0	0	0	0	0
100	32	32	29	24	16
150	96	94	87	75	59
200	160	157	146	129	105
250	224	220	207	185	155
300	287	283	267	241	205
350	351	346	328	297	255
400	415	409	388	353	305

Data: $\sigma_1 = \sigma_2 = 0.4$, $X = 100$, $T = 1$, $N = 2$, $r_f = 0.05$

Results for Figure 44: The Effect of Relative Project Value with Two Design Alternatives

	Option value				
S_1 / S_2	$\rho = -1.0$	$\rho = -0.5$	$\rho = 0$	$\rho = +0.5$	$\rho = +1.0$
0.5	16	16	16	16	16
1.0	32	32	29	24	16
1.5	76	71	66	62	59
2.0	120	113	108	106	105
2.5	163	159	157	155	155
3.0	206	205	205	205	205
3.5	255	255	255	255	255
4.0	305	305	305	305	305

Data: $S_2 = 100$, $\sigma_1 = \sigma_2 = 0.4$, $X = 100$, $T = 1$, $N = 2$, $r_f = 0.05$

Results for Figure 45: The Effect of Project Volatility with Three Design Alternatives

	Option value				
$\sigma_1 = \sigma_2 = \sigma_3$	$\rho = -1.0$	$\rho = -0.5$	$\rho = 0$	$\rho = +0.5$	$\rho = +1.0$
0.1	20	17	14	11	7
0.2	31	27	22	16	10
0.3	42	36	30	22	13
0.4	53	46	38	28	16
0.5	64	56	46	33	18
0.6	74	65	54	39	21
0.7	84	74	61	44	23
0.8	93	83	68	49	25

Data: $S_1 = S_2 = S_3 = 100$, $X = 100$, $T = 1$, $N = 2$, $r_f = 0.05$

Results for Figure 46: The Effect of Relative Project Volatility with Three Design Alternatives

	Option value				
$\sigma_1 / (\sigma_2 = \sigma_3)$	$\rho = -1.0$	$\rho = -0.5$	$\rho = 0$	$\rho = +0.5$	$\rho = +1.0$
0.25	39	37	32	26	17
0.50	43	40	34	26	17
0.75	48	43	36	27	16
1.00	53	46	38	28	16
1.25	56	50	42	32	20
1.50	59	53	45	36	24
1.75	62	56	49	39	28
2.00	65	59	52	43	32

Data: $S_1 = S_2 = S_3 = 100$, $X = 100$, $T = 1$, $N = 2$, $r_f = 0.05$

Results for Figure 47: The Effect of the Underlying Values with Three Design Alternatives

	Option value				
$S_1 = S_2 = S_3$	$\rho = -1.0$	$\rho = -0.5$	$\rho = 0$	$\rho = +0.5$	$\rho = +1.0$
50	0	0	0	0	0
100	53	46	38	28	16
150	123	115	102	82	57
200	194	185	166	139	102
250	266	254	231	197	151
300	337	323	296	254	199
350	409	393	361	312	248
400	481	462	425	370	297

Data: $\sigma_1 = \sigma_2 = \sigma_3 = 0.4$, $X = 100$, $T = 1$, $N = 2$, $r_f = 0.05$

Results for Figure 48: The Effect of the Number of Underlyings and their Volatilities on the Option Value

	Option Value							
Standard Deviation / Number of projects	0.1	0.2	0.3	0.4	0.5	0.6	0.7	0.8
1	10	13	16	20	23	26	30	33
2	10	16	22	29	35	42	48	54
3	14	22	30	38	46	54	61	68

Data: $S_1 = S_2 = S_3 = 100$, $\rho_{12} = \rho_{13} = \rho_{23} = 0$, $X = 100$, $T = 1$, $N = 2$, $r_f = 0.05$

Results for Figure 49: The Effect of the Number of Underlyings and their Values on the Option Value

	Option Value							
$S_1 = S_2 = S_3$ / Number of projects	50	100	150	200	250	300	350	400
1	0	20	66	115	168	220	273	325
2	0	29	87	146	207	267	328	388
3	0	38	102	166	231	296	361	425

Data: $\sigma_1 = \sigma_2 = \sigma_3 = 0.4$, $\rho_{12} = \rho_{13} = \rho_{23} = 0$, $X = 100$, $T = 1$, $N = 2$, $r_f = 0.05$

Results for Figure 51: The Effect of the Number of Underlyings on the Option Value

$\rho_{12} = \rho_{13} = \rho_{23}$ / Number of projects	-1	-0.5	0	0.5	1
1	33	33	33	33	33
2	62	58	54	45	29
3	93	83	68	49	25

Data: $S_1 = S_2 = S_3 = 100$, $\sigma_1 = \sigma_2 = \sigma_3 = 0.8$, $X = 100$, $T = 1$, $N = 2$, $r_f = 0.05$

Results for Figure 52: ENPV as a Function of the Development Process – Linear Costs

$\rho_{12} = \rho_{13} = \rho_{23}$ / Number of projects	-1	-0.5	0	0.5	1
1	23	23	23	23	23
2	42	38	34	25	9
3	63	53	38	19	-5

Data: $S_1 = S_2 = S_3 = 100$, $\sigma_1 = \sigma_2 = \sigma_3 = 0.8$, $X = 100$, $T = 1$, $N = 2$, $r_f = 0.05$

Results for Figure 54: ENPV as a Function of the Development Process – Non-Linear Costs

$\rho_{12} = \rho_{13} = \rho_{23}$ / Number of projects	-1	-0.5	0	0.5	1
1	23	23	23	23	23
2	37	33	29	20	4
3	30.5	20.5	5.5	-13.5	-37.5

Data: $S_1 = S_2 = S_3 = 100$, $\sigma_1 = \sigma_2 = \sigma_3 = 0.8$, $X = 100$, $T = 1$, $N = 2$, $r_f = 0.05$

Appendix 5: Definition of Terms

Term	*Definition*
Competitive advantage	Measured in terms of economic rents
Control	Is the decision rule, which is implied by an optimal strategy
Design alternative	A subset of the total system (auto), e.g., an engine
Development	The process of going through (Ulrich and Eppinger 2000, p. 17): o Concept development o System design o Detail design o Testing
Financial markets	The vector of marketed asset prices
Flexibility	Management's ability to respond to unfolding uncertainty
Model of design	Either point-based serial engineering, point-based concurrent engineering, or set-based concurrent engineering
Module	See "Design alternative"
Optimal	The best solution to a problem given a number of restrictions
Option	The value of flexibility
Real option	A discretionary right , with no obligation, to purchase or sell a non-financial asset for a specified price
Strategic fit	A process of sequential choice: deciding *where* to compete in the market
Strategic stretch	A process of sequential choice: deciding *how* to compete
Subsystem	See "Design alternative"
Term	*Definition*
Sustainable	Long term

Uncertainty	Not being certain about an outcome in terms of expected cash flows. In this case, uncertainty is quantified by the second moment of a stochastic variable
Valuation principle	A technique for finding comparable claims
Value	The price which the financial markets would assign to a comparable claim

Bibliography

Adler, P. S., Goldoftas, B., and Levine, D. (1999), "Flexibility versus efficiency? A case study of model changeovers in the Toyota production system," Organization Science, Vol. 10, No. 1, pp. 43-69.

Adner, R. and Levinthal, D. A. (2004), "What is not a real option: considering boundaries for the application of real options to business strategy," Academy of Management Review, Vol. 29, No. 1, pp. 74–85.

Akao, Y. (1990), "Quality Function Deployment: integrating customer requirements into product design," Productivity Press Inc., IL.

Amram, M. and Kulatilaka, N. (1999), "Disciplined decisions- aligning strategy with the financial markets," Harvard Business Review, January-February, pp. 95-104.

Argyris, C. (1983), "Action science and intervention," Journal of Applied Behavioral Science, Vol. 19, pp. 115-140.

Arrow, K. and Debreu, G. (1954), "Existence of an equilibrium for a competitive economy," Econometrica, Vol. 22, pp. 265-290.

Arrow, K. (1969), "The organization of economic activity: issues pertinent to the choice of market versus non-market allocation," in: The Analysis and Evolution of Public Expenditure: The PPB system. Vol. 1 U.S. Joint Economic Committee, 91st Congress, 1st Session. Washington D.C.: U.S. Government Printing Office, pp. 59-73.

Arrow, K. (1985), "The economics of agency," pp. 37-51, in: Pratt, J. and Zeckhauser, R., eds., "Principals and agents: the structure of business," Harvard University Press, Boston, MA.

Baldwin, C. Y. and Clark, K. B. (1997), "Managing in age of modularity," Harvard Business Review, September-October, pp. 84-93.

Baldwin, C. Y. and Clark, K. B. (2002), "The option value of modularity in design," Working Paper, Harvard Business School, Boston, MA.

Barbaris, N. and Thaler, R. (2003), "A survey of behavioral finance," in: Constantinides, Harris, and Stultz (eds.), "Handbook of the economics of finance," JAI Press, Greenwich, CT.

Bernardo, A. E. and Chowdhry, B. (2001), "Resources, real options, and corporate strategy," Journal of Financial Economics, Vol. 63, pp. 211-234.

Bingham, N. H. and Kiesel, R. (2004), "Risk-neutral valuation – pricing and hedging of financial derivatives," 2nd ed., Springer-Verlag, London.

Black, F. and Scholes, M. (1973), "The pricing of options and corporate liabilities", Journal of Political Economy, Vol. 81, May-June, pp.637-659.

Borison, A. (2003), "Real options analysis: Where are the Emperor's clothes?," Working Paper, Stanford University, CA.

Bowman, E. H. and Hurry, D. (1993), "Strategy through the option lens: An integrated view of resource investments and the incremental-choice process," Academy of Management Review, Vol. 18, No. 4, pp. 760-782.

Boyle, P. P. (1988), "A lattice framework for option pricing with two state variables," Journal of Financial and Quantitative Analysis, Vol. 23, pp. 1-12.

Boyle, P., Evnine, J., and Gibbs, S. (1989), "Numerical evaluation of multivariate contingent claims," The Review of Financial Studies, Vol. 2, No. 2, pp. 241-250.

Brealey, R. A., Myers, S. C., and Allen, F. (2005), "Principles of corporate finance," McGraw-Hill, 8th ed., New York, NJ.

Brodbeck, M. (1968), "Readings in the philosophy of the social sciences – 'Models, meanings, and theories'," Macmillan Publishers Ltd, NY.

Brown, J. S. and Duguid, P. (2001), "Knowledge and organization: a social practice perspective," Organization Science, Vol. 12, No. 2, pp. 198-213.

Bryan, L. L. (2002), "Just-in-time strategy for a turbulent world," The McKinsey Quarterly, Special edition: risk and resilience, pp. 17-27.

Carr, P. (1993), "The valuation of American exchange options with application to real options," Working Paper, Cornell University, NY.

Chandy, R. K. and Tellis, G. J. (1998), "Organizing for radical product innovation: the overlooked role of the willingness to cannibalize," Journal of Marketing Research, November, pp. 474-487.

Childs, P. D., Ott, S. H., and Triantis, A. J. (1998), "Capital budgeting for interrelated projects: a real options approach," Journal of Financial and Quantitative Analysis, Vol. 33, pp. 305-334.

Childs, P. D. and Triantis, A. J. (1999), "Dynamic R&D investment policies," Management Science, Vol. 45, No. 10, pp. 1359-1377.

Clark, K. B. and Fujimoto, T. (1991), "Product development performance – strategy, organization, and management in the world auto industry," Harvard Business School Press, Boston, MA.

Clark, K. B., Fujimoto, T., Ellison, D. J., and Hyun, Y. (1995), "Product development performance in the auto industry: 1990s update," Working Paper, Harvard Business School, Boston, MA.

Coase, R. H. (1937), "The nature of the firm," Economica, Vol. 4, pp. 386-405.

Cohen, W. M. and Levinthal, D. A. (1990), "Absorptive capacity: a new perspective on learning and innovation," Administrative Science Quarterly, Vol. 35, pp. 128-152.

Collis, D. J. (1994), "Research note: how valuable are organizational capabilities?", Strategic Management Journal, Vol. 15, pp. 143-152.

Copeland, T. E. and Antikarov, V. (2001), "Real options: a practitioner's guide," Texere LLC, New York, NJ.

Copeland, T. E., Weston, J. F., and Shastri, K. (2005), "Financial theory and corporate policy," Pearson Addison Wesley, Reading, MA.

Coyne, R. D., Rosenman, M. A., Radford, A. D., Balachandran, M., and Gero, J. S. (1990), "Knowledge-based design systems," Addison-Wesley Publishing Company, Reading, MA.

Cox, J. C. and Ross, S. A. (1976), "The valuation of options for alternative stochastic processes," Journal of Financial Economics, Vol. 3, pp. 145-166.

Cox, J. C., Ingersoll, J. E., and Ross, S. A. (1985), "An inter-temporal general equilibrium model of asset prices," Econometrica, Vol. 53, Issue 2, pp. 363-384.

Cox, J. C., Ross, S. A., and Rubinstein, M. (1979), "Option pricing: a simplified approach," Journal of Financial Economics, Vol. 9, pp. 229-264.

Davis, G. and Parker, C. (1997), "Writing the doctoral dissertation," Barron's Educational Series, Inc., NY.

De Reyck, B., Degraeve, Z., and Gustafsson, J. (2004), "Valuing real options in incomplete markets," Working Paper, London Business School.

Dixit, A. K. (1989), "Entry and exit decisions under uncertainty," Journal of Political Economy, Vol. 97, No. 3, pp. 620-638.

Dixit, A. K. and Pindyck, R. S. (1994), "Investment under uncertainty," Princeton University Press, Princeton, NJ.

Duffie, D. (1996), "Dynamic asset pricing theory," Princeton University Press, Princeton, NJ.

Ellison, D. J., Clark, K. B., Fujimoto, T., and Young-suk, H. (1995), "Product development performance in the auto industry: 1990s update," Working Paper, Harvard Business School, Boston, MA.

Fama, E. (1996), "Discounting under uncertainty," Journal of Business, Vol. 69, Issue 4, pp. 447-458.

Faulkner, T. W. (1996), "Applying 'options thinking' to R&D valuation," Research - Technology Management, May-June, pp. 50-56.

Fisher, I. (1930), "The theory of interest," Macmillan, New York, NJ.

Garman, M. B. (1976), "A general theory of asset valuation under diffusion state processes," Working Paper, University of California, Berkeley, CA.

Geske, R. (1979), "The valuation of compound options," Journal of Financial Economics, Vol. 7, No. 1, March, pp. 63-81.

Geske, R. and Shastri, K. (1985), "Valuation by approximation: A comparison of alternative option valuation techniques", Journal of Financial and Quantitative Analysis, Vol. 20, pp.45-71.

Grant, R. M. (2002), "Contemporary strategy analysis – concepts, techniques, applications," 4th ed., Blackwell Business, Malden, MA.

Grenadier, S. and Wang, N. (2004), "Investment timing, agency and information," Working Paper, Stanford University, CA.

Hagel, J. and Brown, J. S. (2005), "The only sustainable edge: Why business strategy depends on productive friction and dynamic specialization," Harvard Business School Press, MA.

Hall, R. (1993), "A framework linking intangible resources and capabilities to sustainable competitive advantage," Strategic Management Journal, Vol. 14, pp. 607-618.

Harrison, J. M. and Kreps, D. M. (1979), "Martingales and arbitrage in multiperiod securities markets," Journal of Economic Theory, Vol. 20, pp. 381-408.

Häcki, R. and Lighton, J. (2001), "The future of the networked company," The McKinsey Quarterly, Vol. 3, pp. 26-39.

Henderson, R. and Clark, K. B. (1990), "Architectural innovation: the reconfiguration of existing product technologies and the failure of established firms," Administrative Science Quarterly, Vol. 35, January, pp. 9-30.

Henderson, V. (2005), "Valuing the option to invest in an incomplete market," Working Paper, ORFE and Bendheim Center for Finance, Princeton University, Princeton, NJ.

Hull, J. C. (2003), "Options, futures, and other derivatives," 5th. ed., Prentice Hall, Upper Saddle River, NJ.

Hull, J. and White, A. (1990), "Valuing derivative securities using the explicit finite difference method," Journal of Financial and Quantitative Analysis, Vol. 25, No. 1, pp. 87-100.

Iansiti, M. (1995), "Shooting the rapids: managing product development in turbulent environments," California Management Review, Vol. 38, No. 1, pp.37-58.

Jackson, M., Kalai, E., and Smorodinsky, R. (1999), "Bayesian representation of stochastic processes under learning: De Finetti revisited," Econometrica, Vol. 67, July, pp. 875-893.

Jaikumar, R. (1986), "Postindustrial manufacturing," Harvard Business Review, November-December, pp. 69-76.

Jensen, M. and Meckling, W. (1976), "Theory of the firm: managerial behavior, agency costs and ownership structure," Journal of Financial Economics, Vol. 3, pp. 305-360.

Johnson, G. and Scholes, K. (2002), "Exploring corporate strategy," Pearson Education Limited, Harlow.

Kamrad, B. (1995), "A lattice claims model for capital budgeting," IEEE Transactions on Engineering Management, Vol. 42, No. 2, pp. 140-149.

Kamrad, B. and Ritchken, P. (1991), "Multinomial approximating models for options with *k* state variables," Management Science, Vol. 37, No. 12, pp. 1640-1652.

Kogut, B. and Kulatilaka, N. (1994), "Options thinking and platform investments: investing in opportunity," California Management Review, Vol. 36, pp.52-71.

Kogut, B. and Kulatilaka, N. (2001), "Capabilities as real options," Organization Science, Vol. 12, No. 6, pp. 744-758.

KPMG (2006), "2006 KPMG global auto executive survey," Automotive momentum industrial products, January, United Kingdom.

Kulatilaka, N. (1993), "The value of flexibility: The case of a dual-fuel industrial steam boiler," Financial Management, Vol. 22, Issue 3, pp. 271-280.

Laffont, J.-J. and Martimort, D. (2002), "The theory of incentives. The principal-agent model," Princeton University Press, Princeton, NJ.

Leedy, P. D. (1980), "Practical research – planning and design," Macmillan Publishing Co., Inc., New York, NJ.

Lei, D., Hitt, A. H., and Bettis, R. (1996), "Dynamic core competences through meta-learning and strategic context," Journal of Management, Vol. 22, pp. 549-569.

Liker, J. K., Sobek, D. K., Ward, A. C., and Cristiano, J. J. (1996), "Involving suppliers in product development in the United States and Japan: evidence for set-based concurrent engineering," IEEE Transactions on Engineering Management, Vol. 43, No. 2, pp. 165-178.

Linn, R. and Gronlund, N. (2000), "Measurement and assessment in teaching," Prentice-Hall, Inc., 8th Edition, NJ:

Lintner, J. (1965), "Valuation of risk assets and the selection of risky assets in stock portfolios and capital budgets," The Review of Economics and Statistics, Vol. 47, No. 1, pp. 13-37.

Luehrman, T. A. (1998), "Strategy as a portfolio of real options," Harvard Business Review, September-October, pp. 89-99.

Luenberger, D. G. (2001), "Projection pricing," Working Paper, Department of Management Science and Engineering, Stanford University, CA.

Luenberger, D. G. (2002), "A correlation pricing formula," Journal of Economic Dynamics & Control, Vol. 26, Issue 7/8, pp. 1113-1127.

MacDuffie, J. and Benko, C. (2006), "Auto industry consolidation: Is there a new model on the horizon?" Knowledge@Wharton, January 25, University of Pennsylvania, The Wharton School, PA.

Marakowitz, H. (1952), "Portfolio selection," Journal of Finance, Vol. 7, pp. 77-91.

McDonald, R., and Siegel, D. R. (1986), "The value of waiting to invest," Quarterly Journal of Economics, Vol. 101, pp. 707-727.

Merton, R. C. (1998), "Applications of option-pricing theory: twenty-five years later," The American Economic Review, Vol. 88, No. 3, pp. 323-349.

Merton, R. and Bodie, Z. (2005), "Design of financial systems: towards a synthesis of function and structure," Journal of Investment Management, Vol. 3, No. 1, pp. 1-23.

Millman, A. F. and Wilson, K. J. (1994), "From key account selling to key account Management", 10th Industrial Marketing and Purchasing (IMP) Conference, September, University of Groningen.

Mintzberg, H. (1978), "Patterns in strategy formation," Management Science, Vol. 25, pp. 934-948.

Morison, M. (1993), "Methods in sociology," Longman, London, England.

Mun, J. (2002), "Real options analysis – tools and techniques for valuing strategic investments and decisions," John Wiley & Sons, Inc., Hoboken, NJ.

Myers, S. C. (1977), "Determinants of corporate borrowing," Journal of Financial Economics, Vol. 5, pp. 147-175.

Myers, S. C. (1984), "Finance theory and financial strategy," Interfaces, Vol. 14, pp. 126-137.

Ng, F. and Bjornsson, H. (2001), "Evaluating a real option in material procurement," Working Paper, Stanford University, CA.

Nonaka, I. (1990), "Redundant, overlapping organization: a Japanese approach to managing the innovation process," California Management Review, Vol. 32, pp. 27-38.

Pandza, K., Horsburgh, S., Gorton, K., and Polajnar, A. (2003), "A real options approach to managing resources and capabilities," International Journal of Operations & Production Management, Vol. 23, No. 9, pp. 1010-1032.

Papalambros, P. Y. and Wilde, D. J. (1991), "Principles of optimal design, modelling, and computation." Cambridge University Press, New York, NJ.

Peteraf, M. A. (1993), "The cornerstone of competitive advantage: a resource-based view," Strategic Management Journal, Vol. 14, pp. 179-191.

Peteraf, M. A. and Barney, J. B. (2003), "Unraveling the resource-based tangle," Managerial and Decision Economics, Vol. 24, June, pp. 309-323.

Pinches, G. E. (1998), "Introduction: Real options: developments and applications," Special Issue of The Quarterly Review of Economics and Finance, Vol. 38, pp. 533-535.

Porter, M. (1980), "Competitive strategy," Free Press, New York, NJ.

Porter, M. (1985), "Competitive advantage: creating and sustaining superior performance," The Free Press, New York, NJ.

Prahalad, C. K. and Hamel, G. (1990), "The core competence of the corporation," Harvard Business Review, May-June, pp. 79-91.

Pratt, J. and Zeckhauser, R., eds., "Principals and agents: the structure of business," Harvard University Press, Boston, MA.

Pugh, S. (1991), "Total design: integrated methods for successful product engineering," Addison-Wesley Publishing Company, Wokingham, England.

Quinn, J. B. (1986), "Managing innovation: controlled chaos," McKinsey Quarterly, Spring, pp. 2-21.

Rubenstein, M. (1976), "The valuation of uncertain income streams and the pricing of options," Bell Journal of Economics, Vol. 7, pp. 407-425.

Rumelt, R. P., Schendel, D. E., and Teece, D. J. (1991), "Strategic management and economics," Strategic Management Journal, Special issue, Vol. 12, Winter, pp. 5-29.

Samuelson, P. (1965), "Proof that properly anticipated prices fluctuate randomly," Industrial Management Review, Vol. 6, pp. 41-49.

Schumpeter, J. A. (1950), "Kapitalismus, Sozialismus und Demokratie," Munich.

Schwartz, E. S. (2002), "Patents as R&D as real options," Working Paper, Anderson School at UCLA, CA.

Shapiro, A. C. (1989), "The theory of business strategy," RAND Journal of Economics, Vol. 20, No. 1, pp. 125-137.

Shapiro, A. C. (1991), "Modern corporate finance," Macmillan Publishing Company, New York, NJ.

Sharpe, W. F. (1964), "Capital asset prices: A theory of market equilibrium under conditions of risk," The Journal of Finance, Vol. 19, No. 3, pp. 425-442.

Smit, H. and Ankum, L. (1993), "A real options and game-theoretic approach to corporate investment strategy under competition," Financial Management, Vol. 22, No. 3, pp. 241-250.

Smit, H. and Trigeorgis, L. (2006), "Real options and games: Competition, alliances and other applications of valuation and strategy," Review of Fincial Economics, Vol. 15, No. 2, pp. 95-112.

Smith, A. (1976), "An inquiry into the nature and causes of the wealth of nations," Oxford University Press, Oxford, (originally published 1776).

Smith, J. E. and Nau, R. F. (1995), "Valuing risky projects: option pricing theory and decision analysis," Management Science, Vol. 41, No. 5, pp. 795-816.

Smith, J. E. and McCardle, K. F. (1998), "Valuing oil properties: integrating option pricing and decision analysis approaches," Operations Research, Vol. 46, No. 2, pp. 198-217.

Sobek, D. K. (1997), "Principles that shape product development systems: a Toyota-Chrysler comparison," Doctoral Dissertation, Industrial and Operations Engineering, University of Michigan, MI.

Sobek, D. K., Ward, A. C., and Liker, J. K. (1999), "Toyota's principles of set-based concurrent engineering," Sloan Management Review, Winter, pp. 67-83.

Soderberg, L. G. (1989), "Facing up to the engineering gap," The McKinsey Quarterly, Spring, pp. 2-18.

Sorensen, D. J. (2001), "Valuation of R&D investments in a portfolio illustrated using the real options approach," Master's Thesis, Copenhagen Business School, Denmark.

Spear, S. J. (2004), "Learning to lead at Toyota," Harvard Business Review, Vol. 82, Issue 5, pp. 78-86.

Stalk, G., Philip, E., and Shulman, L. E. (1992), "Competing on capabilities: the new rules of corporate strategy," Harvard Business Review, March-April, pp. 57-68.

Starr, M. K. (1965), "Modular production, a new concept," Harvard Business Review, Vol. 43, No. 6, pp. 131-142.

Stiglitz, J. (2000), "The contributions of the economics of information to the twentieth century economics," The Quarterly Journal of Economics, Vol. 115, pp. 1441-1478.

Tallman, S. and Fladmoe-Lindquist, K. (2002), "Internationalization, globalization, and capability-based strategy," California Management Review, Vol. 45, pp. 116-135.

Teece, D. J., Pisano, G., and Shuen, A. (1997), "Dynamic capabilities and strategic management," Strategic Management Journal, Vol. 18, No. 7, pp. 509-533.

Trigeorgis, L. (1991), "Anticipated competitive entry and early preemptive investment in deferrable projects," Journal of Economics and Business, Vol. 43, No. 2, pp. 143-156.

Trigeorgis, L. (2000), "Real options – managerial flexibility and strategy in resource allocation," MIT Press, Cambridge, MA.

Trigeorgis, L., and Mason, S. P. (1987), "Valuing managerial flexibility," Midland Corporate Finance Journal, Vol. 5, No. 1, pp. 14-21.

Ulrich, K. T. and Eppinger, S. D. (2000), "Product design and development," McGraw-Hill, 2nd ed., Boston, MA.

Waites, R. (2002), "Reinventing corporate research," Research – Technology Management, July-August, pp. 15-22.

Ward, A., Liker, J. K., Cristiano, J. J., and Sobek D. K. (1995), "The second Toyota paradox: how delaying decisions can make better cars faster," Sloan Management Review, Spring, pp. 43-61.

Wasti, S. N. and Liker, J. K. (1999), "Collaborating with suppliers in product development: a U.S. and Japan comparative study," IEEE Transactions on Engineering Management, Vol. 46, No. 4, November, pp. 444-461.

Wheelwright, S. C. and Clark, K. B. (1992), "Revolutionizing product development – quantum leaps in speed, efficiency, and quality," The Free Press, New York, NJ.

Wolfe, R. (2005), "Increase in U.S. industrial R&D expenditures reported for 2003 makes up for earlier decline," National Science Foundation, December.

Internet Sources:

http://knowledge.wharton.upenn.edu/article/1365.cfm (accessed on January 15th 2006)

http://www.jdpower.com/pdf/2005088.pdf (accessed on June 1st 2005)

FSC
www.fsc.org
MIX
Papier | Fördert gute Waldnutzung
FSC® C083411

Kolibri 360 GmbH
Ferdinand-Jühlke-Straße 7
99095 Erfurt, Deutschland
produktsicherheit@kolibri360.de